WOMAN RESTORED

From Devastation to Restoration

Barbara King

Copyright © 2020 – Barbara Ann King

All rights reserved. This book is protected under the copyright laws. This book may not be copied or reprinted for commercial gain or profit. The use of short quotations or occasional page copying for personal or group study is permitted and encouraged. Permission will be granted upon request. Unless otherwise indicated, Scripture quotations are taken from the Holy Bible, New Living Translation, copyright © 1996, 2004, 2015 by Tyndale House Foundation. Used by permission of Tyndale House Publishers, Inc., Carol Stream, Illinois 60188. All rights reserved. Scripture quotations marked NIV are from THE HOLY BIBLE, NEW INTERNATIONAL VERSION®, NIV® Copyright© 1973, 1978, 1984, 2011 by Biblica, Inc.® Used by permission. All rights reserved worldwide. Scripture quotations marked AMP are from the Amplified Bible. Copyright © 2015 by The Lockman Foundation, La Habra, CA 90631. All rights reserved. Scripture quotations marked AMPC are from the Amplified Bible, Classic Edition. Copyright © 1954, 1958, 1962, 1964, 1965, 1987 by The Lockman Foundation. Scripture quotations marked MSG are from The Message. Copyright© 1993, 2002, 2018 by Eugene H. Peterson. Used by permission of NavPress. All rights reserved. Represented by Tyndale House Publishers, Inc. Scripture quotations marked NKJV are from the New King James Version®. Copyright© 1982 by Thomas Nelson. Used by permission. All rights reserved. Scripture quotations marked NLV are from the New Life Version, copyright © 1969 and 2003. Used by permission of Barbour Publishing, Inc., Uhrichsville, Ohio 44683. All rights reserved. Scripture quotations marked KJV are from the King James Version. All emphasis within Scripture is the author's own.

Disclaimer: This book contains information that is intended to help the readers be better informed in dealing with change and challenges in life. It is presented as general advice using the author's experience and best judgment but is in no way to be considered a substitute for necessary care provided by a physician or other medical professional.

Published by Eagle's Wings Press.

Publishing services by Evangelista Media & Consulting
Via Maiella 1, 66020 San Giovanni Teatino (CH) – Italy
publisher@evangelistamedia.com
www.evangelistamedia.com

For Worldwide Distribution, Printed in the USA
1 2 3 4 5 6 / 23 22 21 20

Dedication

This book is dedicated to all of the women who have suffered from abuse, addiction, and oppression and have been beaten down to the point of hopeless despair. You are the women who fight daily in the battle to survive and are the champions of life.

There is good news for the oppressed! The prophet Isaiah says in Isaiah 61:1-3,

> *The Spirit of the Sovereign Lord is upon me... He has sent me to comfort the brokenhearted and to proclaim that captives will be released and prisoners will be freed. He has sent me to tell those who mourn that the time of the Lord's favor has come, and with it, the day of God's anger against their enemies...he will give a crown of beauty for ashes, a joyous blessing instead of mourning, festive praise instead of despair. In their righteousness, they will be like great oaks that the Lord has planted for his own glory.*

Acknowledgments

To Dr. Dennis Sempebwa, a lifelong friend, brother, mentor, teacher, encourager, and the one who continually challenges me to go beyond my barriers and step over the thresholds to take me to another level. Thank you for being who God called you to be in my life and standing with me when mud was being flung into my face.

To my dearest friend Ingrid Sempebwa who continually helps me stretch my imagination by helping me to see things from a whole other perspective, thank you. You have stayed faithful through the years and have a heart of the finest gold.

To my mother, Jean, who is my example, who loves with simplicity and truth yet shows strength and perseverance through life's worst situations, coming through it with a heart without hate or grudges and unconditional love. Thank you, and I love you!

To all of my siblings who are indescribable with words to say all of the wonderful things that encompass each one of you, I thank you. My deepest love to all, and God's richest blessings be upon all of you.

To my jewel of a friend Dale Wilson, thank you. It's amazing how simply God brought us together and time has never demolished our friendship; through the good, the bad, tears, and laughter we are connected through this life journey.

To all of my spiritual fathers, counselors, spiritual sons and daughters, teachers, friends, and enemies near and far, I thank you because without every one of you, I would not be who I am today. God bless you all!

Endorsements

Barbara King has delivered with insight, as well as inspiration, a book that surely refreshes. Her wealth in the Word of God floods this book with Holy Spirit insight that can transform the many entanglements and toughest problems that we face on this planet today. Her personal story shows how the timeless truth relates to, transforms, and restores our lives as the process, in time, leads to the promise.

Dr. Phillip Myles
Attorney, Speaker, Pastor
California, USA

This is a horrifying story of innocence stolen and abuse unimagined. But God's love has Barbara in the crosshairs, and it's redemptive power enveloped her, healed her, and allowed her to live a life of testimony and victory. Thank you, Barbara, for sharing your vulnerability and trust in God. What a privilege to know such a giant in Christ like you!

Ingrid Sempebwa
Director, Eagle's Wings International
Texas, USA

A few years ago, I was honored to serve alongside Barbara at a charity event. Almost immediately, God knit our hearts as we compared stories. Like her, I know what it's like to be abused, used, and dropped. I understand the injuries that come from emotional oppression and addiction. *Woman Restored* tells Barbara's graphic story of divine redemption. She provides an easy-to-follow roadmap from despair to restoration, forgiveness to freedom, and faith to maturity. Thank you for this excellent work, Barbara.

Lisa Romesburg
Vice President, The Romesburg Corporation
Chief Operating Officer, Eagle's Wings International
Mission Viejo, California, USA

Woman Restored is the true story of Barbara King, a young girl whose faith in God brought her from captivity to freedom. It is an amazing lesson on overcoming seemingly hopeless situations to living a victorious life. This is a powerful book and a MUST-read!

Dale Wilson
CEO, Omar Supplies
Chicago, Illinois, USA

Woman Restored—what a powerful testimony that takes the reader through her reality walk of victory in Christ! Barbara suffered unyielding victimization and shame by her abusers very early in life—but her resolute belief in Jesus would rescue her and kept her alive to tell her story. *Woman Restored* is a must-read book and will bless anyone seeking or in need of hope, healing, and restoration.

Minister Madlyn K. Williams
Founder, The Fire's Flowing Ministries
Florida, USA

Contents

Foreword by Dennis Sempebwa 11
Opening 13

Chapter 1	Hopeless Homelife..	15
Chapter 2	Freedom Foiled—Justice Prevailed................	33
Chapter 3	Death and Life...	47
Chapter 4	Shame and Wounds and Fear..........................	69
Chapter 5	Faith	83
Chapter 6	Heart Revelation..	95
Chapter 7	Forgiveness..	111
Chapter 8	Renewing Your Mind	121
Chapter 9	Taking Control of Your Thoughts	139
Chapter 10	Repentance..	163
Chapter 11	Salvation	185

Closing... 203
About the Author 207

Foreword
by Dennis Sempebwa

It is almost two decades ago when we first met. We had just stepped off the stage after ministering at an annual conference in her church. "Do you guys have some way for your fans to know what God is doing, and how to keep up with you?" she quizzed. Well, we didn't. Almost immediately, she offered to help us design and manage a monthly newsletter for our award-winning music group.

When that season ended and God called me to launch a Christian university program, Barbara was the first to volunteer. We would build a global network of twenty-two extension campuses in eight countries. When we felt led to plant a church in Chicago, Barbara stepped up again to serve as our church administrator.

When I stepped out of that season to serve the Body of Christ worldwide as an itinerant apostolic minister, she once again stepped up to serve on our board of directors, which she still does today. My wife, Ingrid, and I could not do what God has called us to do without this precious woman of God. Together, we have built ministries, weathered tempests, endured betrayals, and enjoyed tremendous victories.

When I think of Barbara, two words come to mind: tenacity and loyalty. Barbara didn't go to school to learn that life only yields its finest fruit from sustained diligence. No one taught her how to be the faithful and consistent friend that she has proven to be throughout the years. She learned all this the hard way, at the school of experience. Her tempestuous history as detailed in this book gave her the critical life training that has caused her to touch so many people in such positive ways.

Barbara knows pain, despondency, tragedy, betrayal, and loss. She also knows the triumph of conquest that comes from trusting God through it all and allowing the Potter to make the vessel as it pleases Him.

Woman Restored will make you cry, make you mad, and make you sing. Her unrelenting grit and grace is boldly displayed in the pages of this moving book. Barbara clearly introduces you to this overarching thought: *Regardless of your circumstances or history, God is well able to heal, perfectly restore, and use us to impact our world.*

As you read through these pages, allow the power of this story and its lessons to transform you and draw you closer to God's design for your life.

Dr. Dennis D. Sempebwa
President, Eagle's Wings International
CEO, Sahara Wisdom Center
Chancellor, THE 300
Dallas, Texas, USA

Opening

Within these pages is a portion of my story. In simplicity and truth, I hope to share some part of me and how knowing Jesus has changed my life. My prayer is that my experiences would help and inspire every hurting woman to see that the world is not as it seems. There is a better way, and it is possible.

No one is promised a life without trials; actually, the Scriptures teach us that we will have trials and tribulations in this life (John 16:33). Another truth the Bible reveals is that we can go through the fire and come out untouched and without even smelling like smoke. What seems impossible in this broken life, Jesus can pick up all the pieces and put them back together, restoring us to a better life than anything we imagined.

The Lord delivered and restored me to a new person, and I believe that what God delivers us from He then expects us to do that for someone else. People need people, and God works through us to help others. So throughout my life thus far, broken, shattered women have been coming across my path. Some come for a moment, and some come for several years.

Within those relationships, they open up and share their brokenness, and I can share my testimony.

Each woman is different, but the stories of abuse are the same—the same as mine. The love the Lord has shown me, I want to share with other shattered women and give them hope, deliverance, and a direction. Countless numbers of women and men break into tears hearing the true gospel and how much God truly cares and loves them, void of religion, but the simple truth of the gospel.

I am a woman restored by the grace of God. I pray that throughout this book you will see the Bible and God in a different way than perhaps you have learned or heard. He is love and hope, and the Bible reveals Him in glorious personal ways to each of us.

Many today say there isn't enough evidence to show that God and Jesus are real. Yet I know and have witnessed a plethora of evidence all around us every day—living, breathing examples walking around, and I am one of them: a woman restored by the overwhelming love of God. God is my Father, Friend, Counselor, and Mentor. To Him, I give all the praise and honor.

Chapter 1

Hopeless Homelife

And they have defeated him by the blood of the Lamb and by their testimony. And they did not love their lives so much that they were afraid to die.
—Revelation 12:11

"Jesus, please take me back. You made a mistake and left me here. I don't belong here and don't want to be here. Please, Jesus, don't leave me here I don't belong here," tearfully prayed a young girl with all of her being.

That young girl praying to Jesus was me. That was my constant prayer and hope in my heart as a young girl of seven. I only knew the world as I lived it. My home, family, and lifestyle were all I knew of the world. Until I went outside of that realm, I didn't know there is a whole ocean—and I lived only in a fishbowl.

Since the age of six, I had been physically beaten, molested, and verbally abused by my father. I thought everyone lived as we did in our family, until I experienced another way of life when visiting relatives. Only then did I realize the nightmare I was living.

As far as today's standards, we had a relatively large family of six children. I was the third child, oldest girl. My dad was always home, as my mom worked two or three jobs to support her family. None of us escaped the nightmare.

My mom had no love or support. Rather, she was worn down not only from her back-breaking work, but when she was at home, she feared saying or doing something wrong that would make our dad beat her. We all lived that way, in constant fear of saying something wrong or not doing precisely what Dad wanted—knowing we would be punished or beaten.

Being sent to our room was a punishment we all hoped for, because it was safe. Our home was a violent environment. We lived in constant fear. Consequently, we children and our mother were always clean, quiet, obedient, and presentable at all times. Each of the children was assigned chores that were posted on the wall. Once we completed a task, we checked it off the list. Then our dad would double-check our work. If not as spic and span as he thought it should be, we would get whipped and then have to do the chore again.

Even brushing our teeth was stressful. After we would brush our teeth, we had to go to our dad for inspection. He had tablets that we chewed and would turn color on our teeth and show where we missed brushing. If any color showed up, he would hit us and make us brush our teeth again.

Food was scarce for us, but not for our dad. He always had his cigarettes and his favorite foods, like ice cream. After he ate some ice cream, he would mark a line in the container so he could tell if anyone had eaten any. If he thought someone was stealing a bite, we would all get punished if we didn't confess who did it. We didn't know who might have snuck downstairs to get a bite because we were kept apart from each other.

Good food and snacks were only for him. His food came first. The rest of us lived on food like corn mush, pasta, and hominy. If there was no money left for food for us, oh well, we went without. One time, when we lived in an apartment, my dad had leftover pizza in the kitchen. As I lay in bed that day, I could smell it and I was hungry. I quietly snuck out of bed and into the kitchen and lifted the box lid to take a piece. Suddenly, I was grabbed from behind by the throat, and my dad held a gun to my head. He said, "I will not be stolen from! Are you sure you want to take that piece of pizza?" I dropped it immediately. He told me it was best for me to go right back to bed. Needless to say, I never tried that again.

PERIODIC REPRIEVES

My grandparents on my mom's side would help us get food. We didn't have money for school lunches so our grandmother, who lived beneath us, would make lunch for us and then sneak it to us by leaving lunch bags between her door and screen door every morning. As we walked down the back stairs, we would quietly reach between the doors and pick up the bags of food. My dad would never allow charity, and to him that would have been charity, so it was all kept hush-hush. One day he found out, and that was hell to pay.

Sundays after church was our favorite time. We would go to Grandma's home downstairs, and she would make a nice meal. Then we could watch TV together. Dad would never come because he hated people. We loved our grandmother so much—what a gift from God she was to us!

My great aunt, our grandmother's sister, lived across the courtyard with her son, our uncle. They didn't like my dad. They would say they needed our help with stuff at home, that way we could go over to their place and they would feed us and let us play together. That is where I got my love for Christmas. They decorated to the hilt, and food plus candy was everywhere. Until today the beauty of Christmas stays with me. My favorite holiday next to Christmas is Easter. If it weren't for my mom's family, we would not have had any clue about another way of life.

Although we were poor, Mom was able to pay the mortgage on the house so we would have a roof over our heads. There was no money for a car, food was scarce, and clothes were hand-me-downs. We ate what was in front of us, or we did not eat. We knew how to cook, clean, sew, paint, and make minor repairs in the home. Toys were scarce, and playtime was never a thing in our home. We were not even allowed to be together, except to eat.

There was never a time of day when we were free from Dad; since he didn't work, he was always at home. He claimed he was wounded in the navy and could not work for that reason. That meant our mother worked continually to support us all. There were times when Mom was at work on the third shift at the factory, Dad would sneak out at night with his hair slicked back and wearing his black leather jacket.

My mom sacrificed all that she was for us. She had weak ankles and several times during the winter months, she slipped on the ice. One year, she fell and broke her ankle in the middle of winter—yet she would still go to work, taking three buses on crutches.

All of that would be bad enough for any child to endure, but from the age of six to fourteen years old, my father sexually abused me. The abuse was not only sexual but also physical and emotional. There was not a day that went by that I didn't fear for my life.

At home, hiding away in my bedroom with the door closed, my conversations with Jesus were not prayers. Instead, it was begging. I would beg and plead with Him saying, "You made a mistake and left me here. I want to go back." Back where? I wanted Him to take me back to Heaven.

Since none of us children were allowed to play with each other and silence was the golden rule, we were kept separate when Dad was around. There were only a few times he had to allow us to play, and that was with any relatives who may have been in town. Once in a while, if we were good and he felt generous, he allowed us to all gather in the TV room. Otherwise, we were kept separate and confused as to what the others believed or thought.

One of the tools my dad would use to pit us children against each other was on those days when he felt happy and generous and allowed us to watch TV. If one of us did well or was in his favor for the day, he would allow only that child to watch TV, while the rest of us were to be in our rooms. My only solace was to be in my bedroom. I would hide in my room reading a Bible someone from church gave me—until one day my dad got angry with me for reading it and took it away.

There are six of us now, but for a time, it was just my two older brothers and me. We had a tight bond secretly, but we couldn't let Dad know or we would be beaten and punished for talking to one another, especially since I was a girl and they were boys.

My fear was so intense it was difficult for me to sleep. I hoped and prayed every night that my bedroom door would not open that night. School was a refuge, except my mind was so consumed about what was happening or what might happen when I went home, that I had a difficult time learning. I became a child who totally closed up and shut up inside. There was no peace anywhere in my life or my mind, so sleeping only came as I cried myself to sleep, praying to Jesus.

My mom was concerned, so she took me to the doctor's office. After an examination and talk with the doctor, I was prescribed a mild sedative. I didn't open up and tell the doctor anything that was happening to me. That would mean an inevitable beating when I returned home. Would I risk a beating? No way. The doctor said children are not usually given a sedative, but in my case, he thought it best. We went home, and life continued as usual. Yes, normal. I believed that it was normal for children to live with beatings and molestations—no laughing, smiling, or playtime. No vacations, day out to the movies, or a picnic as I learned some families did. We had only chores and school.

Going to school was just as bad because I couldn't focus on anything but going home and facing Dad was worse. I was numb with fear. Maybe you can understand that. I tried to pay attention at school, but all that consumed my thoughts was 3:00 p.m. when I had to go home. And, he timed me.

If I was one minute late, I was beaten coming in the door. Then he questioned me why I was late, who was I talking to, who was I with? My grades were awful. It wasn't that I was unable to grasp the curriculum; I was frozen with fear and didn't listen. I was in my head dealing with fear. Eventually, the teachers put me in special classes because I couldn't keep up.

We were not allowed to have friends, so the other kids at school looked at me as odd. They would talk about me and make fun of me. Some kids who lived on our block knew how mean our dad was. I was so closed up with absolutely no social skills of any kind. I had mastered being seen and not heard with absolute obedience.

A few years we were actually allowed to go trick-or-treating for an hour. But it was too dangerous for him to let us out of his sight for too long in fear that we might tell people what was going on at home. The boys had a little more leniencies since they had no idea what was going on with the girls and there was no threat to dad with them revealing anything, but the girls he kept close.

DEEP DESPERATION

No matter how much I begged and pleaded with God, He never came to get me out of there and take me home to Heaven. Eventually, I got tired of waiting on God, so I planned my suicide. I talked to God and Jesus about it and told them, "If you don't take me back soon, I will kill myself because I want to be with You. I don't want to be here!"

I never heard a response from God; He never answered me. So I planned. I would put everything neatly in order, get ready for bed, then take all the sleeping pills that I could swallow, lay down, and it would be over. I would finally be free; so I was decided and waited for the right time. I did everything just as I imagined. Even today I can feel the emotions and thoughts and be right back there in that room.

One day, I decided it was the right time and I did it. I took the pills, lay on my bed, cuffed my hands on my chest, and closed my eyes to sleep. Forever I will remember the actual feeling of the separation of my body and spirit—and I felt close to leaving my body, except my spirit would not go.

Then I heard the voice of God. He called my name. I didn't answer because I was in a deep sleep and unable to talk, even in my spirit. It is difficult to explain, but the whole conversation was in spirit, not physically. He called again, and I fought myself to respond, but I couldn't move my body or wake from sleep.

Something pulled inside me; it was as if I was forced to respond, but then I realized what was happening and said, "NOOO…don't tell me I can't kill myself!" I was saying this in my spirit.

God said, "You are not going to die, but live for Me."

"No, no, no!" I said.

God didn't respond to my words. Instead He said to me, "Now get up and get a drink of water."

Suddenly, I felt connected to my body again, but I couldn't open my eyes no matter how hard I tried. Yet the moment I felt connected to my body, all the other senses took over, and the room felt like it was spinning uncontrollably, and that was with my eyes closed. I kept trying hard to open my eyes, but they were so heavy, and the spinning made it nearly impossible.

I'm not sure what time it was, but it was night because the house was dark and quiet. I was unable to stand up, so I slid down off the side of my bed, crawled to the door, opened it, and crawled to the bathroom down the hall, feeling the way with my hands on the walls. I went in, closed the door, and locked it. Our bathroom was so small that when I shut the door and sat down on the floor, no one could get in. I fought to pull myself up, which seemed to take forever, and grabbed a Dixie cup. Holding myself up on the sink, I filled it with water and took a sip. It was so cold and refreshing, it was the best water I ever tasted.

The next thing I remember was falling over to the toilet and vomiting. That is the last thing I remember before waking up on the floor as my brother was banging on the door because he had to use the bathroom. I don't know how long I was out, but I was so sick and still felt dizzy and nauseous.

I was barely able to get ready for school, but fear kicked in, and school was safer than home. I only imagined what Dad would do to me if he found out about my attempted suicide. He could see I was sick, but I didn't say anything and kept moving. I went to school and one of the girls in my class, who also lived across the street from me, came over and asked, "Are you okay?" I said yes, but she could see I was lying and stayed by me the whole day.

She was so kind that I finally told her what I did. She somehow understood and comforted me. No one had ever been kind to me, but this girl. And to this day I thank God for her and pray for her. Well, I slowly got better and now had a secret friend at school. It took years before I was able to retake a pill without gagging.

A FEW GOOD MEMORIES

I remember a couple of good memories from childhood. One was Christmas, and the other was the church. Christmas is the best memory because there was so much food in my aunt's home. And in our home, Mom worked extra hard to have the same. There would be fruit, nuts, candies, and turkey for Christmas dinner.

Every child dreams of the gifts they would like to wake up to on Christmas morning. We couldn't afford much, but my mom did what she could with help from her parents. Most of the time, the gifts would be clothes or socks and underwear. Toys were unnecessary in my dad's perspective, but once in a while, maybe. My grandparents, aunt, and uncle sacrificed so much for us despite themselves.

For each other, we would make things. I dreamed of things I saw other kids get, like a Raggedy Anne doll, which at that time was a big deal. But we couldn't afford it, so it never came. We would all try to give to one another, but it was never much. One year, one of my brothers was working and managed to save money to get us all gifts. How he did it, I don't know because if anyone worked and lived in the house, they had to give their paycheck to Dad. One year my brother gave me a brand-new camera—it shocked me to have something new and beautiful. Dad, of course, took it away from me because I "didn't need it." I always remembered that Christmas.

When I was older, my brother learned I always wanted a Raggedy Anne doll and a Barbie doll. So even as an adult, that is what he gave me for Christmas. I still have both today. It's those small acts of kindness that still mean a lot to me. They listened, remembered, and took time to get me a gift with their money. Both of my brothers are the best I can ever imagine having.

Another good memory as a child was going to church. That was a place of safety and freedom. We were raised in the Lutheran religion, and it was there I first heard of Jesus. We all attended Sunday school, and even at the tender age of five, I still remember the day I listened to the Christmas story of Jesus. As the teacher told the story, something excited me inside. To this day, I can see that room, the chair I was sitting in, and the smell in the air. Strange how some things stay with you all of your life. I listened intently to the story of Christmas and Jesus's birth, and without hesitation I believed it and wanted Jesus! That is when I began spending all my time in my room and praying for Jesus to take me back.

As a family, there was no money for Bibles, especially for six children. A Sunday school teacher at church knew we couldn't afford it, so she bought Bibles for us. I was so excited about having my own Bible, that to this day it is almost in pristine condition. That gesture was life changing for me, and I'm not sure she ever knew how great a gift it was to me.

The pastor of the church was big into children. He had his own and also adopted a couple. He would have events for the kids all the time. Something was always going on at the church for kids. The pastor knew we had a troubled home life, and we were not allowed to have friends, play, or be gone for too long. Somehow he worked out a plan, saying he needed us to serve at the church, which work was something Dad would agree to. When we arrived at church ready to work, the pastor took us to the fun events. We went to the beach, had campfires, played block tag, and ate. It was a place of refuge, and we were so thankful to God for him!

Through the kindness of the pastor, we got to play with the other children in the neighborhood. One game we would play was block tag. On the side entrance of the church there were iron gates that would lock by a pole dropping into the ground. One night we were all playing block tag on the church block and I ran around the corner chasing the pastor's son to tag him. I slipped and fell and my mouth hit the metal pole and busted open my front lip and broke a front tooth right down the middle. The pastor and I had to come up with a story so Dad wouldn't know we were playing.

Another person took an interest in us children at church—the choir director. One of my brothers and I have good singing voices. The choir director started a children's choir, and we both sang in it. Her profession was voice training during the week in the downtown lyric opera building. She noticed something special about my brother and me, so she wanted to train our voices for free and place us in the adult choir. We were the two youngest in the choir ever! My mom was in the adult choir too for a time.

The choir director told me I could sing all eight octaves and made a big deal out of it. She said I had a wonderful soprano voice. I remember going to her apartment for training, and it was gorgeous! She had red hair and a personality that lit up the room, very bubbly and outgoing—the opposite of me. I struggled with training because I was a deep introvert. How could she say I was so good when all I heard at home was how useless I was? She stayed with it and wanted me to go to operatic school; but of course, Dad said absolutely not. "What a waste of a voice," she said. Nevertheless, it would never be.

I sang my whole young life. As I got older, the director had me train with all of her other students and charged $25 per lesson, which was a steal compared to what others paid. Twice she got my voice to crack the glass, which is an amazing accomplishment. Because my self-esteem was at zero, her encouragement didn't register. My first solo at church was "Beautiful Savior." I had so many compliments that never sank in because I didn't believe them.

The pastor convinced my dad to allow me to attend vacation Bible school. I was not big on playing the games outside, so I sat on the sidelines. One day, one of the team leaders sat next to me and talked about all kinds of things. With compassion and understanding, he said at the end of game time, "One day everything will get better and you will be great! Everything will be okay." I thought it sounded wonderful, but just a wish.

So I have good memories at the church we grew up in—my only experience of being a child and socializing. In my early teens, church became my second hideaway. Unfortunately, I was taught religion rather than the love of God, which created more fear and bondage in me than freedom. God sounded just as fierce as my dad. It seemed God was angry at how horrible we were as people, but He would love and accept me if I was a good girl. I thought that if I were like the women in the Old Testament, God would love and accept me, and then I would have worth.

I was obedient as a child, quiet and teased as a goody two-shoes. It was true, except they didn't understand that I was petrified with fear that set a course of trying my utmost to be good enough for God to love and accept me. I can still hear my plea to God, "I will be good, please love and accept me. I know I am no good, but I will be. You will see."

God was good to us even then, as you have read, just as fierce except the rewards were nicer. He placed people in our lives who gave us a way of escape. If even for a short time, it was wonderful. I only had religious teaching, so my understanding of God as the Father was similar to understanding my earthly dad. I felt afraid to make Him angry. I heard the phrase, "You better watch it, or God will get you." So religion kept me in chains too. There was no freedom, just more rules and regulations with the threat of punishment not only in this life but hell to come. I certainly didn't want that, because I wanted to go to Heaven, not hell. So I didn't want to make God mad at me too, like my dad, and end up worse off for eternity.

Jesus was loving and kind, that I could understand; but God is also a Father, and my understanding of father only came from my dad. That fact mixed with the Old Testament stories they taught us in Sunday school, which made me fear God just as much.

CONTINUING PATTERN OF ABUSE

Life never got better, and God didn't come for me. Nevertheless, I kept believing and praying. My demeanor was completely shut down. I didn't talk. I was always unhappy, and I didn't even eat much. I just went from day to day in a stupor.

One day I came home from school and went upstairs. I could hear my sister crying in her bedroom. I went in to see what was wrong and she told me what Dad did to her. I don't even have words to describe every feeling that was going on inside me. I held her as she cried. Desperately I wanted to protect her from this ever happening again. I accepted my fate, but not for her. So I promised her, "Don't worry, I will make this stop so he will never do this again." From that day forward, I was determined to protect my sisters from Dad's sexual abuse torture.

My only idea was to run away. I thought that if Dad focused on me being gone, the others would be safe. He was so afraid of any of us talking about how he abused us. I prayed about it and continued to wait for just the right time. Then, the opportunity came unexpectedly. It was my night to do dinner dishes and it was a beautiful summer night, so the back door was open. I could feel the wind blow through the screen door as I washed the dishes. My sisters were in their rooms, including my dad. Mom was at work, and one of my brothers was good, so he got a reward to watch TV. He was the only one on the first floor.

While I was washing the dishes and listening to the TV, in my spirit, I heard "GO NOW!"

"What?"

"Go, now," the voice said again.

"Oh my gosh, no, my brother will hear me and I will get caught."

"Just go, I will protect you," I heard.

So I stopped washing the dishes, dried my hands, and quietly tiptoed to the back door. The old-style screen door was made of wood, so it squeaked as I opened it slowly and slid through. We had a long, fenced yard with a garage in the back, right before the entrance to an alley. My heart was beating so fast and I was scared, but I tore off running through the yard and into the alley. I stopped, frantically thinking, "Now what?"

A few doors away was an apartment building that had an open stairway with porches. I ran up several flights and hid in a corner. Terrified, I wondered what I should do next. At that point, it was too late to change my mind. I knew that once they realized I was gone, they would search for me and also call the police. I just waited until I knew what to do next.

After a short time, I saw people looking for me, they were going up and down the alley, but I stayed still and quiet, crouching back into the darkness. Finally, I heard, "Go now." But where? I had no idea, but I ran down the alley and got to the main street. I started walking toward my oldest brother's place who lived on his own. I can't say how many miles I walked down that main street late at night all alone—I was only 14 years old at the time.

I ended up walking to our old neighborhood, where my aunt and grandmother still lived. My mom had eventually saved enough money that she bought a home for us all and we moved out of the small apartment. But my grandmother and aunt still lived in the apartment complex.

As I was walking, a police car drove by me going the opposite direction. I thought for sure he saw me, but he drove right past me. I walked faster and turned off the main street to the side street right by my aunt and grandmother's building. Suddenly, my older brother drove up in his car; he was looking for me and had a hunch I would go there.

He took me to his apartment, sat me down, and asked why I ran away. Of course, I couldn't tell him everything. We were all beaten, so he understood that part, but he felt something else was wrong. I couldn't say. The embarrassment and shame, let alone the fear were too much. Then his phone rang, and it was Dad. My brother said, "Yes, she's here." I'm not sure all that was said on the phone, but when he hung up, my brother was scared.

"I will have to take you home, but in the morning. It's too late now," he told me. Neither of us slept well, and in the morning, we were both quiet all the way home. Fear was gripping us both.

As we approached the house, he stopped the car and said, "I don't want to do this, but I have no choice. Something is wrong, but you're not telling me what it is." As we got closer, we saw Dad was waiting outside for me. Mom was standing inside the door, waiting. She was angry, but glad I was home. She hugged me when I walked into the house and said, "Your dad is angry." By that time he was standing not far behind her.

All the other kids were upstairs in their rooms being quiet. It was not a good day for me. And I made their day bad too. My thinking was, "I failed and got sent back." My dad took me aside to grill me about what I might have said about him. He threatened me and anyone I would run to if I ever thought about running away again. My brother, aunt, grandmother, anyone, he said, he would have them arrested if he found me at any of their homes. I couldn't bear it if anyone got hurt because of me, so I had to come up with another plan. I already decided to run away again, but the grip was even tighter now, if that could even be possible.

Chapter 2

Freedom Foiled— Justice Prevailed

The time came and I graduated from grammar school and was now a freshman in high school. I had to take public transportation to the high school since it was miles away from home. My brothers' grades in grammar school were very good, so they were accepted into a top honor high school. I went to the other high school for average kids.

Being so far away from home, it was easier for me to talk to people without getting caught. I made friends with two sisters who loved to dance. Disco was big then. Music and dance was something I loved too, so that built our relationship and we started a small dance group. The three of us would dance during lunch breaks at the local restaurant where all the high school kids would go. Our bond was so tight we felt we would always be together.

I came to learn they were unhappy at home too, and that similarity brought us together even more. We would ditch school and go to their home to hang out while their parents were at work. Being friends, we talked all about our personal lives at home, and one day they said to me, "We've decided to run away, come with us."

Wow. I listened to them, and they had it all planned. The plan seemed good, so I agreed. Well, it didn't go as expected, and we all got caught. The police found us and took us to the high school principal's office. Our parents were called. My second oldest brother was sent to get me from high school and take me home on the bus. As we were riding the bus home, I frantically told him why I couldn't go back and all that was going on.

He was under the impression that I was just a "Daddy's girl" because Dad always had me by his side—and my brother hated that. I tried hard to explain to him why, but he said, "What do you want me to do? I'm not going to get beat for you if I don't bring you home." That was the end of the conversation. We all feared for our lives. I couldn't blame him. I didn't want him to be hurt because of me either.

After arriving home and as I took my punishment, Dad said to me, "If you do this again, I don't care who is around, I'm going to slice your throat when you walk through that door." I believed him. I wanted to die, except not by his hand. Nevertheless, I ran away again. I was resolved within me to stop his abuse, even at the risk of death.

I ran to the old neighborhood by my aunt and grandmother's place. I sat down on the steps of another apartment building, looking at their place and remembering what my dad said. So I sat there wondering where I could go or what I could do. Then, behind me came a girl I had gone to grammar school with when we lived in that neighborhood. Cookie was the tough bully in school, a tomboy. One day we got into a fight at school, and I won, and since then we got along.

Cookie happened to be living in the building where I was sitting. She was staying with her grandmother at the time and asked why I was there, so I told her. We sat and talked for a long time and finally she said, "You can stay with me at my grandmother's place tonight if you want." I agreed. I slept on the couch; and for the first time, I felt safe. The next morning she took me out to meet her friends—who were gang members. I ended up hanging out with them that day. She asked them if I could stick around and they said yes. I never joined the gang, but they let me stay with them.

I learned a lot from the gang—loyalty, family order, how to steal, drugs, drinking, pack guns, and a very different way of fighting. Of course, my dad taught me to fight, but this was a different type of fighting. As we were hanging out one day, the leader said to me, "I don't usually do this, but somehow when Cookie asked me, something inside told me I had to protect you. But you do what I say and don't go where I tell you not to go."

I was naive to the ways of the world, and he knew it. I would sleep in empty buildings, party all night, join in some of their fights, and pack guns for them. At that time, the police could not pat down women, since there were no women police officers. I ended up meeting one of the top leaders, Savage, and we started seeing each other. I felt safe with him for the first time in my life. He would take me to the lake for a picnic, and we would talk all night. I never felt so safe as

I did with him. He was so tough but with me such a gentleman and very open. We knew everything about each other.

I still never joined the gang, although the ladies from the gang wanted me to, the leader called them off. I was the other leader's lady, and that was all it was going to be.

After about three months of living on the street, a group of us, Cookie, me, Savage, and a few others from the gang talked about going to California and starting a new life of our own. So we began to plan.

THE TRUTH

The morning we were meeting up at our location preparing to depart for California as I walked down the street with the others, a van came racing toward us, suddenly screeching to a stop. The doors flew open, and a bunch of guys got out with bats and chains. Typically when cars came screeching up, we all took cover in case it was a drive-by shooting. This time it was my brother and his friends. My oldest brother had jumped out and grabbed me and pulled me into the van.

My boyfriend was at work, so he wasn't there. My brother asked some of his friends to help him get me. The van speeded away and then dropped my brother off with me and we went in his car to a restaurant. His girlfriend at that time met us there. He said, "Okay, what's going on? Why do you keep running away? I can't help if you don't tell me."

I knew if I told him Dad would harm him, so I said it was better for me just to run away and not tell him. He had me blocked in so I couldn't get out of the booth. He said, "We are not leaving until you tell me." His girlfriend and I went to the bathroom and she encouraged me to speak to my brother and promised they would protect me. They didn't understand they couldn't, I told them frantically, terrified that they would call him. My brother said the police were looking for me, everyone was scouring neighborhoods for me, and Mom was frightened.

Finally, I broke down and hysterically told them both why. As soon as I told him he said, "I knew it! This is the missing piece of the puzzle!" And it was what he feared. They took me back to his apartment. The next day we went to a restaurant close to where my mom worked. He called her and told her to meet us there. He never told dad he found me.

Mom came and was so mad at me, but then after hearing my brother and me, she was scared. My brother said, "We need to stay here and call the police," which we did. I was in that restaurant for the whole day. My mom, brother, and the police planned how to get my dad. Now I was afraid the police would get hurt because of me. My dad had a gun in the house, and I remembered his words to me if I ran away again. I said to the police, "You don't understand, he will get very violent!"

They said, "Don't worry. Bring the rest of the children here. Do not let them go home. Everyone should stay here while we go and arrest him." The plan was to call him and tell him they had me at the police station, and that he had to come to get me and verify I was his daughter. The police drove to the house, and Dad came out with his black leather jacket and got right into the squad car. As soon as he walked into the police station, they arrested him.

During this time, my brother, mom, and I went to the school to pick up my sisters and we called my other brother at work and told him what happened. We told him not to go home until he heard it was safe. The girls were terrified as we all piled into our brother's small Mustang. My brother questioned them all and asked if what I said was true. The fear in that car was so thick it could be sliced. They both denied it! The baby was still too young, so nothing happened to her, yet. One was screaming at me, another crying, and another silent.

My mom looked at me and said, "If you're lying, I'm going to kill you!" My brother was smart enough to say, "Well, whoever is telling the truth we will find out soon because we are going to the doctor now for an examination. And he will tell us the truth." As soon as he said that, the girls both broke down and said, yes it's true. We went to the doctor, and my mom was afraid of what could be wrong with us. I only know what he said to my mom after my examination and consultation with the doctor and nurses. He said, "Whatever you do, this girl's nerves are shot, she can't get upset or she could break." And yes, that confirmed my mother's fears that we were molested, all except my youngest sister who was fine.

Then, we all had to go to the police station. They separated us and interrogated us one by one. After all of that, they told me I had to face my dad and accuse him face to face. What a horrifying thing to do, but I stayed silent, expecting to be killed. It was a small office with a desk and two chairs. The investigator was sitting behind the desk and my dad was in a chair, handcuffed. Then I had to sit next to him. The investigator asked the questions, and I answered.

They said, "Look at him and say what you told us." He had to tell me a few times, and finally with complete fear, I looked at Dad and accused him of molesting us. They then took him away.

I don't know how the word got out, only that the newspaper reporters showed up at the police station and wanted to know the story. My mother was traumatized by the whole scene, standing there not knowing what was up or down. My oldest brother walked up and told them to please keep it quiet since it was such a traumatic time for us. Any story like this was big news because it wasn't prevalent during this time. Child abuse no doubt happened to others, but things like that were kept secret back then, behind closed doors.

We were assigned an attorney since my mom could not afford one. At 14, I was too young to take the stand but because I was the accuser, they got special permission for me to take the stand. But they could not get the approval for the other girls due to their young age. The case would have to be won based on my testimony alone. The nightmare only began from that moment on.

THE NIGHTMARE'S SILVER LINING

The grilling, preparing me for court, and then going home was far from peaceful. Everyone was afraid and angry at me for telling the truth. All I knew to do was keep walking forward and take my consequences. I was good as dead anyway, because if I lost the case, both my mom and dad would kill me. My brothers and sisters would destroy what was left over. My brothers never went against me, silently they seemed to stand by me. My sisters were the opposite.

One court day after another came and went, and my dad's lawyer was a female. She ripped me apart with no compassion. She accused me of seducing him, dressing seductively to tempt him, and so on. My dad sat there in confidence with a courtroom filled with strangers, looking at this blond-headed lawyer hurling lie after lie at me.

Finally, I lost it. I screamed at her to stop! Stop the lies! I pretty much had a breakdown on the stand. The judge told her to stop, and he tried to calm me down. He asked for the bailiff to get me some water and Kleenex. Then, he called for a recess until I was back in control. I ask you, how does a 6-year-old seduce a man, let alone dress seductively?

Standard procedure after a court hearing was to meet in the lawyer's office and go over how it all went. One day the lawyer met with us afterward and said, "Look, it has come to her word against his. If we do not have more proof, I fear we will lose the case." Silent in the back seat of my brother's car all the way home with my mom in the front seat, she was silent too. My brother said, "There must be something else we can do. Some sort of proof. Think. What could there be?"

I was so consumed inside telling God, "I'm going to lose, they don't believe me. I'm dead." Suddenly, within me I heard, "The black trunk."

"THE BLACK TRUNK," I screamed out before thinking.

My brother said, "What?"

Dad's black trunk was in his bedroom and always locked, and no one was allowed to touch it, not even Mom.

"That's where I saw him put his diary and the pictures. He kept a diary of everything he did, and then he took pictures of us and kept them," I said.

Without thinking twice, I said something horrifying, but true. Somehow the desperation to win the case won over my emotions. We raced home and broke open the black trunk. It was all there and more. Humiliation and shame swept over me as my mom and brother picked up the pictures.

Shockingly, we discovered that Dad was living under an alias name. He changed his name and had paperwork, newspaper clippings, and a great deal of information about his other life, including a wife and children. Could a wife be anymore demeaned than what my mom took that day? With outrage, we contacted the lawyer and told him we had the evidence.

At the next court session, the lawyer presented the evidence to the judge. After glancing at it, the judge dismissed the trial for that day so he could go through the evidence alone. At the very beginning of the next court session, the judge made a statement. The judge looked at me and then the only thing I remember him saying was, "I began reading the diaries and had to stop after reviewing some of them." He said he counted at least ten times my dad attempted to kill me, and the abuse was undeniable.

He asked my mom to stand and asked if she wanted anything. She said, "Yes, a divorce." He granted it on the spot. My dad didn't look so confident anymore.

I was still afraid, ashamed, humiliated, and every emotion was engulfing me. Suddenly, it was over and we won!

I didn't feel like a winner; my only thoughts were, "They finally believed me, someone believed me." He was sentenced to prison, but in a mental ward where he would be evaluated for his mental stability. I felt relieved but still numb.

GANG LIFE REVISITED

The man I was dating while living on the street came to see me and told me he wanted to get out of the gang. He had reconciled with his dad and now was going to work with him, straighten out his life so we could marry. If you know anything about gangs, you know you do not get out alive. Once you take the vow, you are in for life. Because of the favor he had with the leader of the gang and my favor with him, he agreed to let him out of the contract. That was all God.

Unfortunately, his younger sister got caught up in the gang, and when he went to bring her home from a party, a gang leader called him a traitor and then pulled out his gun and shot him dead in the chest. I had no idea this happened until some of the girls came to the theater where I was working and showed me the newspaper clipping. My heart sank, and I certainly felt responsible. His dad was so distraught he said in the news article that we were all forbidden to attend the funeral. I was devastated.

Remember the girls from the gang who wanted me to join but I kept refusing? Well, one day Cookie contacted me and said, "Your sister is at it again. They want to beat her up and have her surrounded at the schoolyard." So I ran to the schoolyard, but it was empty. Then Cookie came out to meet me and said, "Listen, you have to join the gang. These girls are mad." I told her the gang life was not me, and the answer was no. Then out of every corner came the girls and they surrounded me. They said, "You're going to join us, like it or not!" I still refused.

Then, one girl said, "All you have to do is take a hit from each of us and if you don't fall, you're in."

"No," I said.

Then one girl came up and punched me in the face, then another, and one after the other they hit me in the face. I never fell, and they were stunned. I still said, "No, I'm not joining," and walked home. I was swollen and bleeding, and when I walked in the door and went to the kitchen for ice, my sister and brothers saw me and my sister screamed, "OH MY GOD, what happened to you? We need to get you to a hospital!" I told them what happened and said I couldn't go to the hospital.

Not long after that, all the girls from two districts of the gang showed up at my house with bats, knives, chains, and guns. They were outside screaming for me. I was in the back of the house, so I didn't hear them. Suddenly, my oldest brother came running in saying, "They're here for you!"

"Who?" I asked.

"The girls from %@*%&$! gang. You have to run out the back and I will distract them."

A calmness came up inside me, and I said no, I would face them.

"Are you crazy? They will kill you!"

I looked at my brother and said, "What do you want me to do, continue to run?" So I went out on the front enclosed porch and talked through the door. They hurled every obscenity at me and said, "Who do you think you are? Do you think you're too good to join us?" They were there to force me to join or die. I went back and forth with them explaining myself. Then the police came and they all scattered—and they never bothered me again. That part of my life was finally finished.

THE PSYCHOPATH

A short time later, my mom received a call explaining the results of Dad's mental evaluation. He was diagnosed as a psychopath. She was told that he could easily cut your daughter's throat and turn around and have an ice cream cone and think nothing of it. I had no doubt he could; we all had no doubt.

My family didn't know all the horrible things he used to say in private to me. If I did nothing and life continued as it was, he planned on making me his wife when I turned 18 and leave my mom. He said no woman was ever good enough, so he created his own—me. I said I wouldn't marry him. But for my 18th birthday, he said I would have two options: one to marry him or he would kill me because he wasn't going to let anyone else have me.

After he went to prison, he wrote to all of us individually, still claiming his innocence and how I was evil. All of his letters to me were filled with hatred, so I stopped reading them. Some of my siblings kept them and held on to his claim and said it was all me, even though they knew the truth. Fights in the house got worse, as they attacked me for ruining their lives. One screamed that he didn't do anything wrong. "I was okay with what he was doing," she said.

The letters made things worse, and I felt as if my punishment would not end because of the way my sisters felt. But in my heart, I knew I would do it all again because they don't know what I know. And how could they even understand what their future was going to be if he wasn't stopped.

Then the court assigned us to a psychologist who honestly didn't help. In the meantime, my dad contacted his sister and told her what I did. We never knew anyone on his side of the family. Suddenly, his sister came to the house and talked to my mom. She said scornfully, "Which one of you accused him?" They all looked at me; and if looks could kill, I would be dead.

Not long afterward, as all of us were sitting in the dining room talking, my mom at work, the phone rang. I got up and answered it, and it was as if someone punched me in the chest as I heard the most terrifying voice on the other end of the phone, my dad. He was out of prison, his sister paid his bail, and now he was coming for me. Thankfully, my mom got a restraining order against him, so he could not come near me.

The nightmare started all over again, while I was still 14 years young. My brother helped me get a job by lying about my age, and I worked with him at a theater. We did what we could to help mom pay the bills. We took a bus to work. My job was at the concession stand, and my brother was an usher. There were several counters where movie goers ordered food and beverages. One counter was by the front doors made of glass.

As I was working with another girl one day, I looked up and across the street by the bus stop was my dad staring at me. I froze and said, "There's my dad." The girl ran to get my brother, and he ran over and told me to get out of sight while he called the police. The police came and put him in custody and from there he went back to jail. I came to find out he had been following and stalking me—and that day he decided to get me.

After that, my brother and I moved to another theater.

Chapter 3

Death and Life

Jump now three years later. At the age of 17, I met and married my husband. My only dream was to be the best wife and mother I could be. Shortly before that, my menstrual cycle caused extreme pain and excessive bleeding. After an examination in the hospital, it was thought that I was full of tumors. A laparoscopy revealed that there were no tumors but I was suffering from severe endometriosis. They performed a successful surgery. I was prescribed a birth control pill for six months. After that I could stop taking it, and we could try to get pregnant.

After charting and scheduling sex for a few months, I finally got pregnant. Everything was going normally, and it was time for my first ultrasound. I was getting big pretty fast, and because twins run in my family, the doctor thought I might be having twins. A couple of days before the appointment, I began to bleed. We contacted the doctor who said it was normal and not to worry, but I was to stay off my feet. My husband and I went to the ultrasound appointment, happy and excited.

During the examination, the technician couldn't immediately find the baby's heartbeat. Then she said, "Oh here it is." We saw it on the screen, but her face looked puzzled. She called in a doctor and then that doctor called another doctor. All three of them stared intently at the screen.

"What it is?" I asked, "Please don't tell me something is wrong with my baby."

After they discussed it among themselves, the doctor told us that the baby was growing in the fallopian tube, which may burst. I was immediately taken into surgery. If the tube burst, it would put me and the baby at risk of dying. Panic struck us both.

The doctor said for us to go home, get a bag ready, and we would be called when a room was available. My mind was going crazy. I couldn't allow them to kill my baby, it is a sin. Finally, I cracked and said, "I am not allowing you to take my baby!" I argued and refused. They tried to reason with me, but my answer was, "No, I will die with my baby."

The doctor looked at my husband and said, "She is in shock and incapable of making the decision for herself, so you need to make the decision. If she doesn't have the surgery, both she and the baby will die."

Of course, my husband said to do the surgery. We went home and packed a bag, and as we sat in the house waiting, I felt like a failure. "A woman who could not have a baby was worthless," that is what I was taught. As we sat in the living room waiting for the call, my husband sat with his head in his hands and said, "Why me?" I apologized again and again and knew it was all my fault.

After we received the call and were in the hospital, the doctor began to talk to me about the surgery. Again I pleaded with him, "Please don't take my baby." He said, "I have to take care of your life. If you don't go through with this surgery, the tube will burst and we risk losing you too."

I pleaded more and then asked, "Can you take the baby and place it in the right place? Please, please try!" I was so distraught and reaching for any hope at all. He agreed, but I remember the look on his face—he was pacifying me.

I was taken into the operating room. It was a dangerous situation that would take a number of hours to complete. Another woman was having surgery as well. Both husbands were in the waiting room eager to hear the results. A doctor came out and said to my husband, "I'm sorry, she didn't make it." He was devastated. But soon after, a nurse came out and told the doctor, "No not that husband." The nurse reassured my husband that I was okay. The other husband lost his wife. I was fine but I lost a lot of blood and was severely anemic and extremely weak.

The endometriosis had damaged one tube and created a kink; that is where the baby was and was growing and feeding off of the scar tissue. They had to remove the tube, ovary, and baby. After surgery, I was in a recovery room and my husband stood looking out the window. He wouldn't even look at me. I told him I was so sorry. I knew it was my fault and I could understand if he wanted a divorce. He never came to visit me at the hospital again until the doctor called him and reprimanded him. "Don't you understand," he told him, "she has no hope and will die if you don't come?" He was right, I had all those feelings again—I wanted to die.

All was lost! I felt worthless as a woman who could not give her husband a child. Even though he finally came to the hospital to visit me, I felt his disconnect. He came but said nothing. The doctor explained to us what would be necessary after I went home. He said, "When she goes home, she has to lay flat for three weeks for things to heal. She can do nothing, otherwise the stitches may break and she will bleed. She may have to come back for another surgery." The procedures were not as advanced as they are today.

After the doctor left, my husband said, "Just so you know, I can't take care of you when you get home. I have to work." I said, "That's okay, I'll take care of myself." And I did. Our relationship was never the same again. He blamed me and had every right to. Finally, I returned to work where I engulfed myself and was promoted. Our marriage didn't survive and we ended up divorcing.

UPS AND DOWNS OF LIFE

And at that time, I knew nothing of a loving, heavenly Father, I had only "religion"; so according to what I was taught, I was worthless as a woman and a shame to God. Not only was I unable to have a baby for my husband, now I was divorcing, which God hates. After my family found out about the divorce, they rejected me. If that was not enough, I had to move out, and my husband blocked me from the checking account; therefore, I was without money.

I had nowhere to go and everyone was on my husband's side. I was going to have to live in my car. I didn't know how to do even that at this point, so I ended up at my oldest

Death and Life

brother's home begging for help. He reluctantly, against his wife's wishes, took me in.

As the days went by, I grew weaker physically because I slept very little and worked very hard. All the while, I was tormented mentally and spiritually because now I was divorced; and as far as I understood, God disowned me, just as my family did. Consequently, I spiraled down fast listening to all the voices beating me down. I wanted to die again; but now I was convinced I would go to hell. I thought there was no hope for me.

This agony went on night after night, which turned into months, until one night, crying uncontrollably, I said out loud that I couldn't take it anymore. Immediately I heard an inner voice counteracting the voices in my head telling me, "Ask Jesus, call out to Jesus. He will deliver you." I argued and said what a shame I was. The voice kept saying softly for me to call on Jesus to help me.

Finally, I cried out, "Jesus, if it's true and there is anything You can do with my life, it's Yours. I have nothing left. Do whatever You want, just make this stop!" That is the last thing I remember until I woke up in the morning.

When I awoke, everything was different. Suddenly, it was quiet. I had *tremendous peace and quiet and joy*. I felt different inside. I got up, got dressed, grabbed my Bible, and drove to work. During lunchtime, I went to the local park and began to read the Bible. As I opened it and fumbled through the pages of the New Testament, I stopped at 1 Corinthians and began to read. This time it was different, it was as if the words had a voice and spoke to me. Then, I found a radio station that played Christian music and began listening to that on my way to and from work. It was a 45-minute ride, so it became my treasured times.

From there, my life took an about-face. I helped my brother and his wife maintain their home by cleaning and cooking. I slept better and better, and my health began to return. I started to soar at work. Every time I opened the Bible, it spoke to me, and so my hunger grew. I took every word as gold and believed it wholeheartedly.

I read 1 Corinthians 7:11 (NIV): *"She must remain unmarried or else be reconciled to her husband."*

"Oh, here is the answer," I thought, "to correct my mistake of divorce. So that is what I will do!" It turned out my ex-husband missed me too, and we got back together. Now I was succeeding at work, and to him I was more beautiful than before. He started saying rather frequently, "You are too good for me; someone is going to come along and steal you away." I assured him it was not going to happen, but he couldn't get past it. He ended up having an affair, and our relationship broke off again.

Nevertheless, I continued and grew in the Lord. My ex-husband eventually tried to reconcile after realizing he made a mistake. We had a long talk, forgave each other, and became friends. He ended up marrying the other woman and had the children he always wanted.

ANOTHER CHANCE

Eventually, I met another man, married, and wanted to have a baby. Unfortunately, the endometriosis kept returning and there was scar tissue. I went to a specialist.

At this time, I was listening to a preacher on TV who was teaching how healing was part of a believer's salvation. I took that word, and by faith, I stood outside the doctor's office and stopped and prayed, "Lord, if this is true that You died for not only my sins but also sickness and disease, I thank You that all of the endometriosis is gone, in Jesus's name."

The specialist performed exploratory surgery to see what was going on inside. After the surgery when I woke up, he said, "I went through your charts, saw the x-rays, and read through all the notes from the other doctors, but I cannot find one trace of endometriosis. I saw scar tissue that was binding your intestines to your stomach and cleaned that up. Otherwise, I would swear in any court that you never had it—that is how clean it is."

I sat still thinking, "Don't mess it up by saying anything, the Lord healed me, and I don't want to lose it!" The doctor said there was absolutely no reason I could not have a child with one fallopian tube. "Your uterus is slightly tilted, but we can work with that, it just might take longer." So my husband and I began with charting and shots and a scheduled sex life. I was excited!

I was healed by God, and there was no reason for me not to get pregnant! My husband was just as enthusiastic at first—then after a while, he didn't seem so excited. In the middle of this process, he decided he wasn't going to allow another child to be taken from him, so he avoided me altogether. His previous wife had custody of his son, and he had part-time visitation, and the thought of another situation like that made him call off the process. I was devastated. I told the doctor and stopped the treatment. Either way, I carried on, as God's will would be done.

My husband's son from his other marriage was a sweetheart, and we hit it off almost instantly. So much so that he talked about me all the time to his mom after he went home. She got so upset, according to my husband, that she threatened to keep his son away from him. Therefore, I had to stay away from home when my husband's son was visiting him. I don't think the boy understood what was going on, but it broke my heart. Even the boy's grandmother would yell at me if I got too close.

One day, as my husband and I were riding in my car, I was driving and he was in the passenger's seat. I brought up the subject of his son. He immediately screamed that it was none of my business and hit the back of my head. Suddenly, blood was everywhere, gushing out of my head. He was wearing a ring that cut into my head.

I panicked and I pulled over. He got into the driver's seat, and I got into the passenger's seat. I put my head down between my legs, but the blood kept gushing. I thought I was going to die. He drove home crying and saying how sorry he was. When we finally reached home, I ran to the bathroom and put my head over the tub. He came in to see how bad it was, and at that point, I started to get dizzy.

I told him that I needed to go to the hospital, but we had no insurance. He begged, "Please don't call the cops. I'm so sorry." He ran across the courtyard to our neighbor's home and brought them over to our place. The wife was a nurse. She said, "She needs a doctor and stitches." He begged them too, "Please, please help!" She called the doctor she worked for, and they rushed me to the office. The wound required twenty-five stitches in my head.

The doctor asked what happened and my husband answered for me. The doctor asked me if that was true and I agreed out of fear. That was a mistake on my part. At home I was terrified of what would happen next. My husband called his parents and said we were walking, and I slipped and hit my head on the ground. He called my brother too, and as we were talking, I wanted to ask him if I could come to stay with him, but my husband was standing over me so I was afraid to ask. No one ever knew the truth. I regretted that decision.

HOPE AGAIN

My husband was trying hard to be good to me, and I never saw that violent temper toward me again. We continued serving at church, and life seemed to get better. I was still heartbroken about not having a child, until one day at church the pastor said there was an opportunity to help an orphan from Russia. He explained that a family was needed to take the orphan into their home and commit to taking her to the doctor, supporting her through surgeries, and caring for her. There was a sign-up sheet from which the church leadership would pick a family. My heart was so hopeful, and I convinced my husband to sign up. I certainly would take her, and perhaps this was what God wanted me to do. And we were chosen!

The child from Russia was a 14-year-old orphan girl with severe scoliosis of the spine. Without surgery, she would die. She was bent over, and even though her internal organs were still growing, there was no room for them to do so normally. Eventually, she would suffocate and die. Shriners Hospitals for Children volunteered to do the surgery for free if a family would host her. When she arrived, she came with a nurse, and they stayed with us. This young girl and I hit it off immediately. I began to teach her basic English so she could go to school. We enrolled her in school, and she thrived! Even at church, she was loved!

In Russia, the law permitted adoptions only until the age of 15. After 15, they close that door, place the child in another location, assign a job for life, and she would be labeled as handicapped for the rest of her life. So my husband and I talked, and we wanted to keep her and adopt her. We went through the whole process for adoptive parents and dealt with the ministry that was her liaison between Russia and the United States of America (USA). Whatever it took, we wanted to keep her. This was around Christmas, and it would be her first-ever celebration. We planned to make it great for her!

Finally, it was time for her surgery. We were told that she may not be released in time to be home for Christmas, but we continued to plan. We would bring everything to the hospital for her and then have a second celebration when she came home. After the surgery, she had to relearn many things, so I spent a lot of time at the hospital helping her adjust.

SUDDENLY AWRY

Suddenly, things went awry. The ministry kept asking us for more money. Long story short, I found out the ministry promised the young girl to three other families and was bargaining for the best bid. I talked with the church pastor and then exposed the scam wide open! I involved the hospital, our church, and the Russian consulate. The woman head of the ministry was so angry, she tried to take the girl out of the hospital in the middle of winter while she was still in a body cast. When we found out, we and the doctors and nurses hid her—and the devious plan failed. We began communications with Russia with the help of doctors and our pastors. Thankfully, the Russians we spoke to liked me and did not like the ministry head, so they refused to take her calls.

The woman head of the ministry argued with our church and us and told us that the bottom line was that she held power over the girl. This was true as she had the papers that gave her all power. Right before Christmas, she came to the hospital in the middle of the night with her power of attorney over the child and forced the hospital to discharge the child into her custody—even though she was still in a body brace. We were devastated.

Now the Russians had people searching for the girl and we were too. The hospital had no control, but they were just as devastated. After months and no sign of the girl, one day the ministry's personal assistant contacted our pastor saying everyone was so outraged at what the head woman had done to this young girl that they decided to turn on her and the assistant disclosed the location where the girl was being held.

The pastor contacted us and said they found her! The ministry staff walked out, told authorities where the girl was, and the ministry ended up having to shut its doors. Russia was so upset about the whole travesty that the ministry head was ordered to be taken to the Russian consulate immediately, along with the young girl. We contacted Russia and they apologized, but it had become an international incident. The young girl was going to be taken back to Russia.

Thankfully, the ministry's personal assistant told the children's pastor what was happening and set a time for us to show up at the airport so we could say goodbye.

We ate our last meal with her and said goodbye. We tried hard to get her back with a school visa, but to no avail. I sent her money, stamps, and care boxes, but she never received them. She thought we gave up. We learned the government restricted any of our mailing from reaching her. Somehow though, I received some of her letters and would write back. Some started to get through to her, but not all of them.

Soon after, we heard Russia shut its door to American adoptions. We never succeeded in getting her back, and communication was cut off. Eventually, years later, we found each other on social media and have been connected ever since. Her life became exactly as they said. She was placed in permanent housing with an assigned job, labeled as handicapped even though now she was standing up straight and perfectly well.

ANOTHER WHIRLWIND

All in all, the orphaned child experience was so wonderful that I convinced my husband to pursue adopting here in the USA. We signed up with an adoption agency. I wanted a child five years old or younger. After all of the evaluations, they struggled with approving us because although they approved of me, they questioned my husband. They never told me why, but eventually we were accepted and placed us on the waiting list. My hope renewed of having my child. The first was so wonderful, and I imagined another orphan to be the same. I kept hoping and praying.

One day, we received a call from the adoption counselor who told us of a boy who was about to go into the system unless they could find instant parents for him. "The system" is the child protection system, where the children go to a temporary home where assigned parents would take care of him. The system is full of nightmare stories and that wasn't anything I wished for any child.

A Christian family who had other children of their own had already adopted this boy, but after one week, the mother demanded he be taken out NOW! We agreed to go and meet him and the current parents. He was a handsome boy, lively and a charmer. The mother would not say what went wrong, and we couldn't ask. The father was not there. However, the siblings were around.

After the meeting, my husband and I went to dinner. I looked at my husband with longing eyes and asked, "Well, what do you think? He's not a baby, but this boy needs help, and I would hate to see him go into the system." He agreed, "Yes, let's take him." Within a week, I prepared a bedroom, and we went to court to transfer parental rights. We now had a son—a perfect child, for six months.

This time was a whirlwind of joy for me. Because he was from a different country, I began to teach him English. I finally felt complete. Having a son stopped all the talk from my family and friends who felt sorry for me not being able to have a child.

After six months, everything went awry. Six months after the adoption, we would receive a birth certificate with his new name, the agency visitations would end, the process was over, and he would be ours.

Suddenly, this wonderful boy turned into anything but enjoyable. His attitude changed completely and there was nothing but trouble from him. The school didn't want him; at church he got in trouble all the time; and home life was a nightmare.

My husband couldn't understand and said he was finished with him. He quit helping me with our son. I struggled alone to help him. I fought the school systems and took any help and advice I could get. I kept calling the adoption agency to ask for assistance, but was told that we were one of the lucky couples. The other adoptive parents with children from this particular country were in worse shape. Some of the children had stabbed the parents and set fires in the homes. "We can't help you," we were told.

So many stories I could tell, but eventually I was worn out, broken, and felt alone. The church family was trying to help, but no success. The police wrote him off and said he would eventually be one on their list with a record a mile long. "The kid could care less," they said. I even sent him to a psychologist who said the child should be drugged and monitored 24/7, institutionalized, and has no hope.

That angered me, so I argued with him, except this doctor played both sides. He infuriated me, and I was paying him! He told my son he had more rights than his parents, and if he didn't want to do anything, he didn't have to; and if we spanked or punished him, he could call the Department of Children and Family Services (DCFS).

My son eventually gathered a group of kids and convinced them to kill us! His reasoning? He didn't want to have to go to school or obey rules. One thing this boy loved to do was talk.

From the moment he woke up until he fell asleep. I would listen while he talked, and one day he let out by accident his whole scheme. I told my husband and insisted he go to school, have them call the police. They did just that, and the principal and police gathered the kids and they all confessed. My husband and son came home, and the whole story was true, but he didn't file a police report because they worked it all out.

TROUBLE COMPOUNDED

Our son's behavior grew worse, and my husband didn't bother helping in any way. Then the problems tripled when my husband's parents moved in with us. He didn't consult me, just moved them in. His mother exclaimed that she was taking over the household. His dad was dying and soon to be bedridden. As if that wasn't enough stress, around Christmas his dad was on his last days with hospice, my son was out of control, I looked like a train wreck, and I found out my husband was living a double life!

Then the IRS showed up at my door with a letter in hand to evict us from our home—right before Christmas. They froze all of our accounts.

At this time, I had my own thriving business and paid my taxes, yet they froze my account too. I confronted my husband, and he acted as if it was no big deal. I ended up seeking counsel with the pastors and then going to the IRS office and begging for mercy. I had no money, and my husband avoided it all and left me to deal with it. He lived as if nothing was wrong. I eventually worked it out for the IRS to unfreeze my account since I paid my taxes. Eventually, I worked out a deal with the IRS and got his debt reduced from $140,000 to $20,000. And he didn't go to prison.

"Unheard of!" the pastors exclaimed to me. "How did I do it?" they asked. I only knew it was all God—He gave me favor and mercy. Even though I didn't have a clue how to do it and couldn't afford an attorney for him, I filed bankruptcy in his name and business and then provided for my family and his ailing parents.

Between my husband's and son's problems, my body began to show sickness. I went to the doctor, explained every symptom, and said something was definitely wrong. I thought perhaps I was going through menopause early in my 30s. Finally, the doctor set me straight. She said, "You are perfectly healthy. It's not you, it's your environment! Get out of that environment!"

But I was stuck!

My marriage got worse, my husband was cracking mentally, and my in-laws hated me because my husband and son said all of their problems were my fault. Not to mention at this time, I was leading the Ministry of Helps at church and also decided to attend Bible College, working on my Master's degree. I was worn out and beaten down; but again, the church was my refuge. I focused, organized, and determined to get through it all with God's help.

My husband's father died during this time and one day after morning church, we came home and my son went upstairs by Grandma. I went into the kitchen to prepare lunch, and my husband sat down on the couch. He sat with his head in his hands, completely silent. I looked at him, but kept making lunch. Finally, I walked over to him and said, "Are you okay?"

"No," he said without lifting his head. Then he kept repeating, "I'm going to hell.

I'm going to hell…"

I tried to console him and asked him if he wanted to talk about it. He suddenly jumped up and started screaming, "I'm sick of you! Why did you help me through that IRS debt, you embarrassed me! I'm going to kill you!" He started to shove me around, and I kept backing up. I tried to run out to the garage and leave, but he blocked me and cornered me in the laundry room. We are both, at this time, a brown belt in karate, but he had twice the size and weight of me, so it's kill or be killed in my mind.

He grabbed me by the throat and pushed my head back by a window, which I could have gone through. I fought him off, and he backed off and glared at me and came again. I screamed, "Stop! If you come closer, I will have to fight to kill, and we both know how to do it, so stop!" In my mind, I was reconciling the fact that I would let him kill me because I couldn't live with myself if I killed him.

No one from upstairs came down to help me — the house was completely quiet except for my husband screaming, cursing, banging, and mumbling all the bad things he had done. I couldn't understand a lot of what he was saying. I tried to calm him down. "Whatever it is, we can work it out, or we can get you help."

He said, "I need help."

I said, "Okay, let's work on that," trying anything to calm the situation. He finally broke down and sobbed like a baby. As he fell to the floor crying and saying sorry, I looked for the diamond from my wedding ring that broke off as he shoved me. I can only tell you I was as calm as a tree with no wind.

I sat him down, talked to him, made food, and then we got ready to go and serve at church that evening. I was the director of ministries, and my husband and I led the teams for service. I simply had to show up. We drove to church, our son went to class, my husband began his duties, and I got service started.

Then suddenly I stopped, leaned on the counter in the hallway, and began to shake uncontrollably. I couldn't stop shaking and struggled to breathe. I had a panic attack. People came over to help me, not my husband. I asked for my college dean, who attended there and asked if I could speak to him. I told him what happened. We talked through the service. Finally, I decided not to go home with my husband, I'd go to a hotel. People were close by as I told my husband it was better for me to stay at a hotel because I felt threatened. He didn't fight me. That was the beginning of the end.

The marriage fell apart; my son and I are estranged. Now I'm living on my own and working and going to college. I continued to serve at the church, participated in some mission trips, finished my Master's degree and graduated with high honors. My thesis became a book and a college curriculum, which not only got me through a tough period in life but also gave my life a new purpose.

NEW PURPOSE

As life changed, I left that church and became a church administrator with another church. Then, I had the privilege of becoming a part-time associate professor at an extension campus for my alma mater university. Shortly after that, the economy went sour, and I had to close the business and return to the workforce, and was having a hard time. I was at the point where I had enough money to pay for my rent or child support, and so I chose to pay my rent. Although I was three months away from completing child support, I had to make a choice.

My ex-husband took me to court for failing to pay and said, "I don't care if she starves, she needs to pay me my money." The court agreed with him, so I needed to find a job. People refused to hire me based on the fact that I had owned my own business. They thought that eventually I would leave their job to focus on my business. I prayed, "Lord, You know I need a job. I don't want to answer to my ex-husband or owe him anything. I will take any job. Just help me, please."

I finally stopped at a local Walgreens and applied. The female manager asked me what I was doing there with a resume like mine. I explained, and left thinking I would need to prepare to go to a woman's shelter. Before I made it home, the manager from Walgreens called and said I could start tomorrow. I was stunned, but thankful. Of course, it would not be enough income to make it and pay for my child support, so I called the pastor and his wife of my church, who were close friends of mine and explained the situation. They invited me to live with them, but I just couldn't bring myself to do it.

I thought, "God knows where I am, so I'm surrendering to Him and accepting my fate." Two hours later, the pastor's wife showed up at my door with food and a shoulder to cry on. Today, I can't tell you how I made it through those years, I just kept my face to the grindstone and worked side jobs if I could, and never lost hope that God would get me to a better place.

That job at Walgreens led to another and then another and finally another to where I am today. Never once did I quit serving the Lord and kept teaching on Saturdays. Today, I have my own home and live in peace, single, and happy. I know inside God is not finished with me yet. Jesus has done great work in me.

NEVER ALONE

You may think that God didn't take care of me. Why didn't He rescue me from those situations? From my perspective, He did take care of me. Whenever I asked for help, He was there. He never promised to take us out the situations, only that He would make a way of escape.

Jesus Himself never had an easy time on earth, but He would pray and keep walking forward, keeping His eyes focused on the path ahead and never looking back. He was with me sharing every step, every tear, every doubt, and every fear. If it weren't for Jesus, you would not be reading this book. There just are not enough words to describe all that He has done and brought me through. I can say that during all of the challenges and bad times, I pursued Him and the Word more. During the valley of the shadow of death, Jesus kept me, taught me, and carried me through.

I am a restored woman. God took me from devastation to restoration. You might say, "But you didn't get your dream." No, I have a better dream that came to pass. Isaiah 54:1-6 was one of the Scriptures the Lord gave me during those days, and my heart is so thankful:

> *"Sing, O childless woman, you who have never given birth! Break into loud and joyful song, O Jerusalem, you who have never been in labor. For the desolate woman now has more children than the woman who lives with her husband," says the* LORD. *"Enlarge your house; build an addition. Spread out your home, and spare no expense! For you will soon be bursting at the seams. Your descendants will occupy other nations and resettle the ruined cities. Fear not; you will no longer live in shame. Don't be afraid; there is no more disgrace for you. You will no longer remember the shame of your youth and the sorrows of widowhood. For your Creator will be your husband; the* LORD *of Heaven's Armies is his name! He is your Redeemer, the Holy One of Israel, the God of all the earth. For the* LORD *has called you back from your grief—as though you were a young wife abandoned by her husband," says your God.*

My heavenly Father brought numerous people across my path whom I helped to hold on to faith, trust the Lord, heal, and eventually move on to their next station in life.

There is no doubt I have made many mistakes, but God took them all and turned them all around to work out for the good. When I strayed, He never scolded me; rather, He gently guided me until I got right back on the path. If you are a parent, you know that if you remove every obstacle from your children's path and correct every mistake they make, you will undoubtedly set them up for failure. We cannot always allow our children to escape consequences and or issues of life. We love them, no matter what. Right or wrong as they may be, we never abandon them, they are our children.

We can be there to help them through the challenges life brings, but ultimately they have to walk it out for themselves. For example, if your child commits a crime, you will forgive them, but they still have to take the responsibility themselves and face the consequences of their actions. We cannot take that away from them.

God is your loving and forgiving Father, and when you make a bad decision, He will say, "Okay, let's walk through the consequences and/or the pain together."

Chapter 4

Shame and Wounds and Fear

We do this by keeping our eyes on Jesus, the champion who initiates and perfects our faith. Because of the joy awaiting him, he endured the cross, disregarding its shame. Now he is seated in the place of honor beside God's throne.

—Hebrews 12:2

One of the friends of fear is shame. I say this because we don't feel shame without fear. Shame is a painful feeling of humiliation or distress caused by the consciousness of wrong or foolish behavior. It is feelings of humiliation, mortification, embarrassment, discomfort, and sometimes torture.

Today, shame is the second major hindrance in coming to the Lord, next to fear. Fear makes you feel unwilling to move forward or toward something or someone; and shame makes you think that others may look down on you, and you will be rejected.

Do you feel shame? Shame can come for a myriad of reasons. It can be unconfessed sins, an event, or circumstance. Your mind will convince you that everyone who looks at you knows full well what you did. You begin to walk with your head down; and as you walk, there is a feeling that people are whispering about you. Shame imprisons people, and they feel as outcasts, unacceptable, worthless, humiliated, and embarrassed. So they shut down and cower inside, keeping walls up so secure that no one even gets close enough to get in. Inside, they are all bottled up and tightly wound—all the while weeping inside and wishing it would all go away.

Any of that sound familiar? It was familiar to me. For a long time after the truth was revealed, I felt that way. Although I heard all the words that it wasn't my fault, and indeed it was not, nevertheless, I still felt shame.

Shame is nothing new. It began with Adam and Eve in the Garden of Eden. When they ate the fruit of the tree of the knowledge of good and evil, they knew they were naked and hid from God. In Genesis 3:11a, God asked, *"Who told you that you were naked?"* Genesis 3:7 tells that they felt shame: *"At that moment their eyes were opened, and they suddenly felt shame at their nakedness. So they sewed fig leaves together to cover themselves."*

Before that moment, they didn't have any shame and didn't know they were naked. It was the beginning of the conscious. Their consciousness made them realize they were naked. Not the devil. Not God. Once they ate the forbidden fruit, they suddenly became aware of right and wrong. They felt the need to hide from each other and God. They disobeyed God (Genesis 2:16-17) and sinned against God.

Don't we do the same thing today? When you sin, pride can make you want to cover it up, and shame makes you want to hide. Shame keeps us hidden away from people, and it also will keep us away from God. We even fail to confront it ourselves by hiding behind other things, keeping busy to avoid facing our sin. Even if we are Christians and attend church, any secret sin makes us feel shame, thinking that if others knew, they would despise and reject us.

Jesus will never cast you away. He will not reject you as some may or have already done in this life. Don't let shame stop you from approaching Jesus. He is your Restorer.

Luke 5:12 tells a story of a man with leprosy:

In one of the villages, Jesus met a man with an advanced case of leprosy. When the man saw Jesus, he bowed with his face to the ground, begging to be healed. "Lord," he said, "if you are willing, you can heal me and make me clean."

Leprosy is a condition of shame. Today, to be isolated can seem like bliss. Oh, if I could stay away from people, I would be happy. But back in the Old Testament time, everything was about community. If you had leprosy, you were cut off from the community where people did life, and you were forced to live outside of the community. Lepers were cut off not only from people but also from God's presence. Leviticus explains how lepers were to act: *"Those who suffer from a serious skin disease must tear their clothing and leave their hair uncombed. They must cover their mouth and call out, 'Unclean! Unclean!'"* (Leviticus 13:45).

If leprosy wasn't bad enough, they had to cover their mouth as not to spread their germs, then proclaim to everyone around them, warning them to stay away because they had this disease. They were labeled and had to accept their shame.

When Jesus came to town, a leper man out of desperation broke all the rules. He went to Jesus, fell to the ground, and begged to be healed. He said, "Lord, if You are willing." The leper came to Jesus just as he was and asked to be healed.

How did Jesus respond? Read the next verse to find out: *"Jesus reached out and touched him. 'I am willing,' he said. 'Be healed!' And instantly the leprosy disappeared"* (Luke 5:13).

Whoa! Jesus didn't say that the man had to do 12 things and then come back to be healed. Jesus didn't condemn the man by listing his sins and making a spectacle out of him in front of a crowd. No. Jesus did the unthinkable. He reached out and touched him and said, "I am willing, be healed." Jesus touched the leper man—and He touches us when we go to Him and ask to be healed.

Shame can make us feel cutoff! It can make you feel as an outcast! Condemned! We may stay away from Jesus because we fear He will reject us, scorn, or ignore us as people in the world do. We question if Jesus is willing. There were a few times I felt ashamed, and that feeling made me stay away from Jesus temporarily. The fear and shame made me think Jesus would be unwilling—in reality, that's what society taught me—when rather, I should have run to Him. Jesus is more than willing to heal us without condemnation.

THE SHAME OF TAMAR

The shame of Tamar is one I can relate to and perhaps you can as well. You can find the full story in 2 Samuel, chapter 13.

Tamar was the daughter of a king and she had a bright future, which had been stolen from her against her will. Tamar's brother, Amnon, raped her. Someone she trusted, a brother, who instead of protecting her, defiled her out of his selfish desires. He betrayed that trust with absolute disregard for her, her life, his family, or even his father the king. Second Samuel 13:18-19 records what happened to Tamar after this terrible incident:

> *So the servant put her out and locked the door behind her. She was wearing a long, beautiful robe, as was the custom in those days for the king's virgin daughters. But now Tamar tore her robe and put ashes on her head. And then, with her face in her hands, she went away crying.*

I can feel the pain that Tamar felt. Within minutes she went from a beautiful young princess to damaged goods. She was marked for life and filled with shame and disgust. After being thrown out, she tore her clothes, threw ashes on herself, then covered her face, and cried. That one moment in time changed her life forever. I want to scream out loud for her and beat her brother. There wouldn't be enough soap or hot water to clean off the filth or the sickening feeling left from his abuse.

Thankfully her other brother, Absalom, came to her rescue. He took her in and gave her life.

Tamar felt her life was over; and if it had not been for Absalom, it might have been true. Thankfully, Tamar was able to have a full life. The same is true for us. What happened is horrific, but there is still life ahead. We do not have to hide and live in the shame and devastation of it.

The enemy will use shame to keep us shattered and broken. He relies on fear and shame to keep us hidden in the darkness of despair. We are keeping the secrets of what others have done to violate us. If that is you, your story is not over yet! We have the Redeemer, Jesus. If we allow Jesus's love to shine on those dark places and bring it to the light, He is able and will bring redemption, freedom, and restoration to us.

You can overcome the shame as you grow and as you are strengthened in your walk with the Lord. The Holy Spirit assures us of the love that Jesus has for us. My prayer for you is what Paul prays in Ephesians 3:14-19:

> *When I think of all this, I fall to my knees and pray to the Father, the Creator of everything in heaven and on earth. I pray that from his glorious, unlimited resources he will empower you with inner strength through his Spirit. Then Christ will make his home in your hearts as you trust in him. Your roots will grow down into God's love and keep you strong. And may you have the power to understand, as all God's people should, how wide, how long, how high, and how deep his love is. May you experience the love of Christ, though it is too great to understand fully. Then you will be made complete with all the fullness of life and power that comes from God.*

WOUNDS

He [the Lord] heals the brokenhearted and bandages their wounds.

—Psalms 147:3

People who are wounded can draw on the sympathy of others. They do not even have to try; it is the nature of people to want to reach out and help the wounded. A wound will attract people who want to reach out to you and even touch and feel it; and at that point, you may not be ready for anyone to see or touch your wound.

Be sensitive to people with wounds; even though you may want to touch, see, and feel it with them, they may not be ready. When you reach out, they may retract and avoid you. They are telling you they are not ready. Just take your time and love them. Eventually, it may be they will allow you to get close enough to share their pain. Consider Psalms 147:3, 6 (MSG): *"He heals the brokenhearted and bandages their wounds. …Our Lord is great, with limitless strength; we'll never comprehend what he knows and does. GOD puts the fallen on their feet again and pushes the wicked into the ditch."*

Once a wound heals, it turns into a scar. The scar means your wound is healed. You can still see where the wound was, but the skin bound it up and grew new skin over it. When the Lord heals you in any area of life, it should always remind you of God's goodness. There are scars on my body; and when I look at them, I am reminded of what God has brought me through. At the moment, it felt like it would never heal. God can and will heal the wounds of yesterday if you allow Him to. Once the wound is healed, then you may allow people to see and touch your scars. You are willing to let people see the scar left from the wound.

As I look back and see the scars from yesterday, it brings me to tears and thanksgiving to God because I am not there anymore. He healed every wound. Each is a reminder to me to never forget what God brought me out of.

My cautions for you: Be careful who you allow to come close to know your wounds and scars. If you allow the wrong people to come too close to you, they will use the pain of that wound to hurt you again.

EMOTIONAL WOUNDS

Also, emotional wounds need to be healed. I don't know one person who has not suffered from some emotional injury. We all need healing in this area. Even the apostle Paul suffered from emotional disruptions.

Do you have the symptoms of emotional woundedness? The symptoms can range from feelings of hopelessness, self-loathing, irrational expectations of other people, being easily frustrated, hard to feel loved, lashing out, finding it hard to forgive, anger toward God, irritability, being oversensitive about a past situation, a feeling of pain inside that never goes away, and or little to no tolerance. There are many more symptoms, but do any of those describe you?

When we are not feeling well in our physical body, we look for ways to feel better—perhaps go for a walk, cut back on junk food, etc. But when it comes to our mental and spiritual selves, we don't want to take a look at how to fix it.

We know something is wrong, but we don't want to focus on it too long. Maybe there's too much pain. Maybe we don't even realize that there is something unresolved in our past causing us to behave this way. Matthew 26:41b (NIV) says, *"The spirit is willing, but the flesh is weak."*

Emotions are the flesh. When our spirit tells us we need to forgive, our flesh will say no! This is another wound that you cannot heal on your own. Jesus can help you. He is the One who restores us.

Learn to be honest with yourself. Ask yourself who it is you hate or blame in life. What did they do to you? It could even be that you did something you deeply regret. Whatever, emotional wounds need to be healed.

Some ways to help you begin healing is to get into the Word of God, the Bible. I recommend you

- study God's Word;
- meditate on the Scriptures;
- confess known sin to God;
- take control of your thoughts until you learn to walk by His Spirit, not your flesh;
- forgive those who have hurt you; and
- learn to see yourself as God sees you.

None of this is instantaneous. But when you study the Word, wounds will begin to be bandaged and healing will take place.

The personality of Jesus encompasses what He encourages us to be in Galatians: *"But the Holy Spirit produces this kind of fruit in our lives: love, joy, peace, patience, kindness, goodness, faithfulness, gentleness, and self-control. There is no law against these things!"* (Galatians 5:22-23). Further, Hebrews 4:15 says, *"This High Priest of ours understands our weaknesses, for he faced all of the same testings we do, yet he did not sin."*

Remember, Jesus our Lord has wounds. His wounds have become part of our story, and our wounds add to His story. He still has the wounds as He showed to Thomas as told in the Scriptures in John 20:27. It is interesting how God raised Jesus from the dead but didn't take away His scars from His wounds. He told Thomas to touch it, feel it. Jesus still bears the scars of His experience with people here on earth.

His scars serve as a reminder of all that Jesus did for us, and as God was with Jesus, He is also with us. Jesus did not get out of sufferings; He can sympathize with our pain—your pain. Do you suffer from what people do or say? So did Jesus. Were you abandoned and left alone? So was Jesus. Were you condemned unjustly? So was Jesus. When you suffer from loneliness, so does Jesus. And I know that I have not even come close to suffering all that Jesus did—and yet He did it all for us: *"He personally carried our sins in his body on the cross so that we can be dead to sin and live for what is right.* **By his wounds you are healed**" (1 Peter 2:24).

Start by allowing Jesus into the emotions of your hurt memories. He understands the pain of what you have suffered. Jesus is tender, patient, gentle, loving, approachable, and healing. Open up to Him about your emotional pain. Ask Him to help you heal from it and ask Him to reveal who you are to Him and in Him. Remember that He created you, and you are precious to Him. He loves you beyond words, and nothing can separate you from His love.

FEAR

I prayed to the LORD, and he answered me. He freed me from all my fears.
—Psalm 34:4

Don't be afraid, for I am with you. Don't be discouraged, for I am your God. I will strengthen you and help you. I will hold you up with my victorious right hand.
—Isaiah 41:10

So you have not received a spirit that makes you fearful slaves. Instead, you received God's Spirit when he adopted you as his own children. Now we call him, "Abba, Father."
—Romans 8:15

Fear is the number one killer of people today. The definition of fear is terror, fearfulness, panic, dread, anxiety, worry, uneasiness, nervousness, doubt, and suspicion.

Everyone experiences some form of fear in life. Whether it is a scene in a movie, a thunder and lightning storm, or perhaps the fear of losing your job, you have experienced the feeling of fear. Those are emotional types of fear.

A good type of fear is the reverential fear of God. Proverbs 19:23 says, *"Fear of the LORD leads to life, bringing security and protection from harm."* That is not the fear I want to discuss here.

We will examine the fear that cripples and is manipulative. Fear is a spiritual force designed to destroy. This is the type of fear some people have of God, but they shouldn't. He is the opposite of this type of fear. Manipulative fear is when someone forces you or tricks you to do something against your will. God is not a manipulator. Understanding God's love takes fear away: *"**Such love has no fear**, because perfect love expels all fear. If we are afraid, it is for fear of punishment, and this shows that we have not fully experienced his [God's] perfect love"* (1 John 4:18).

The truth is, all fear stems from the fear of death. It is also the number one weapon the devil uses against us. Consider Hebrews 2:14-15:

> *Because God's children are human beings—made of flesh and blood—the Son also became flesh and blood. For only as a human being could he die, and only by dying could he break the power of the devil, who had the power of death. Only in this way could* **he set free all who have lived their lives as slaves to the fear of dying**.

The devil uses the fear of death in many ways to control and manipulate us and to keep us away from God. The devil will tell you every lie to keep you away, such as: God doesn't love, care about, or even want you. We fall for that, but it is not the truth. God desires to have a relationship with us, loves us very much, and has a plan for our lives. The reality is that fear stops us from living. It prevents us from getting to where God wants us to be. Fear is the opposite of faith. Faith is what you needed to get saved—and fear is what stops people from doing so. Don't fall for the devil's tactics.

How can you conquer fear? Stay in the Word, of course. The more you read the Bible, the more you will learn how much God truly cares for you. There are other things you can change in your lifestyle to help, too. First, stop the things that make you fearful. For example, stop or at least lessen the time you watch the news, be careful about what music you listen to, and don't watch horror movies. Learn to guard your heart, eyes, and ears. Fill yourself up with God's Word that produces life, joy, and peace.

Fear is a battle of the mind, and you cannot win the battle thought for thought, you have to win the battle of thoughts with words. What I mean is, you cannot stop your thoughts by trying to think another thought. You have to stop the thoughts by using words. If you are thinking about fear, stop it by confessing Scriptures out loud or singing hymns or Christian songs. Fight the fear battle with your spirit: *"For **God has not given us a spirit of fear** and timidity, but of power, love, and self-discipline"* (2 Timothy 1:7).

That is how to fight the battle when fear attacks you. As you continue to fill yourself up with the knowledge and understanding of the Bible, you will see that it mentions "do not be afraid" and "do not be anxious," approximately 145 times—that is how important it is not to fear. Use faith as a weapon to obliterate fear. Refuse to fear.

We live in a generation where we want things now. In an instant! However, there is no microwave setting to get free from fear. If it were possible, I would have found it. Faith is built; faith comes by hearing and hearing by the Word of God (Romans 10:17) You can't live today on the meal you ate yesterday. You have to eat fresh food today to sustain your health.

It is the same with the Word of God; we need to feed on it daily. It is our spiritual food. We may have had victory yesterday using God's Word, but today we have to refresh, refuel, re-feed our spirit. Fight fear and every issue you have with the Word of God; fight every day as long as you live on this earth.

Chapter 5

Faith

What is faith? God's Word says in Hebrews 11:1 (NKJV), *"Now faith is the substance of things hoped for, the evidence of things not seen."* Let's break this sentence down so we can apply it to our spiritual life.

Faith means you are fully persuaded or convicted based upon hearing, which is belief. Faith is to be totally convinced of something.

Substance is a firm or solid foundation, or confidence.

Hope is to wish for something with expectation of its fulfillment.

When reading the Scriptures, faith rises, and you expect something good to happen. You cannot see it with your natural eyes, but with your spiritual eyes, you can see it. The world calls it imagination and comprehension—but it is more significant than that! It means when you are reading, you can see a movie inside your mind and the words and story become alive. That is why reading is so powerful; it takes you beyond yourself.

You have natural eyes you see with, and you have spiritual eyes that see within you; in conjunction with your imagination, you see the beginning and the end of the story with you in it. When you read the Bible, you can see the words come to life. All of these powerful forces work together, you (who are spirit), Holy Spirit, the Word of God, and your imagination work together, and a beautiful, miraculous thing happens—you see beyond yourself.

The incredible life-giving power of this means that as you read the Bible, the Holy Spirit will speak and reveal to you things you cannot see with your natural eyes (yet) and you believe; and hope springs up that what you see will come to pass in the future. Amazingly, your spirit knows it will, the Holy Spirit agrees with your spirit, and confidence begins to form a solid foundation that it will come to be.

You can read it and apply it in a personal way; right now, I am fully persuaded and convinced with a firm, solid foundation within me and confident with the expectation these things will come to realization. Now Hebrews 11:1 begins to make sense that faith is the substance of things hoped for and the evidence of things not yet seen. That's faith! Romans 15:4 says concerning hope, *"Such things were written in the Scriptures long ago to teach us. And the **Scriptures give us hope and encouragement** as we wait patiently for God's promises to be fulfilled."*

Another Scripture on hope is Romans 5:5 (NIV), which reads, *"And **hope does not put us to shame,** because God's love has been poured out into our hearts through the Holy Spirit, who has been given to us."*

Let's take a look at Hannah in 1 Samuel 1:11 (NIV):

And she made a vow, saying, "LORD Almighty, if you will only look on your servant's misery and remember me, and not forget your servant but give her a son, then I will give him to the LORD for all the days of his life, and no razor will ever be used on his head."

You can find the story in the book of 1 Samuel in the Bible.

Elkanah was Hannah's husband. He also had another wife named Peninnah. Peninnah had no problem bearing her husband children. The Lord closed Hannah's womb. It didn't matter to Elkanah if Hannah bore him children or not because he was deeply in love with her. We can see this love as he gave her a double portion of everything that he had given to his other wife and children. But like most societies, women who cannot bear children are ridiculed, whispered about, and laughed at. That is precisely how Peninnah treated Hannah.

Hannah felt worthless and cried; she eventually became depressed and hopeless. One day after dinner, she went to pray and beg the Lord with the promise. If you are a woman reading this, can't you hear her asking God for a child? Her sorrow was so deep that she went internal. Her lips were moving, but no sound was coming out. Internally, her voice was loud and rose up to the Lord. He hears those deep cries within you that no one else can hear.

The greatest prayer can be a sigh. Our amazing Lord is easily touched by what touches us. Now, many can beg and make promises, but the secret is to follow through on your promises. Hannah did just that and it silenced her mockers.

The Lord remembered her and gave her a son. She followed through and gave her son, Samuel, to the Lord. WOW! She had desperate hope, trusted the Lord, and had *faith.*

People can take you down, mock, ridicule, and judge you to the point where you feel completely broken. Living with no hope, you feel trapped and only wish to be free. The only way to stop the insanity seems to be to die. But no! Don't put your faith and trust in people in the world who cannot do or will even attempt to do anything for you to change things.

Instead, look to Jesus who can change things beyond your most wonderful imagination. No life is worthless. No life is given without reason. God has a plan for you: *"'For I know the plans I have for you,' says the LORD. 'They are plans for good and not for disaster, to give you a future and a hope'"* (Jeremiah 29:11). What seems impossible for you is possible for Jesus!

People wrote me off as someone who had the worse outcomes in life based on what they saw and heard. I should be dead, in jail, living like a beggar on the street, and discarded as trash. And there were times I believed them. It was in desperate hopelessness that I cried out to Jesus. Now those same people are angry with me for succeeding. My life journey has shown me to place my trust in Jesus who is the Author and Finisher of the work He began in me. My life is His; God gave me to Him. My hope and victory are synonymous with the name of Jesus. He is able to complete what He started in you and me—if we have faith and believe and trust Him. Read Hebrews 12:2 (KJV): *"Looking unto Jesus the author and finisher of our faith; who for the joy that was set before him endured the cross, despising the shame, and is set down at the right hand of the throne of God."*

How about faith? Let's think about the father of faith, Abraham. When you read this story in the Bible in the book of Genesis chapter 12, you can see it took a great deal of faith for him to do what God told him to do. God told him to leave everything: family, friends, country—everything familiar that he had known all of his life! He was to go out into the unknown, and God was going to lead him:

> *The LORD had said to Abram, "Leave your native country, your relatives, and your father's family, and go to the land that I will show you. I will make you into a great nation. I will bless you and make you famous, and you will be a blessing to others. I will bless those who bless you and curse those who treat you with contempt. All the families on earth will be blessed through you." So Abram departed as the LORD had instructed, and Lot went with him. Abram was seventy-five years old when he left Haran* (Genesis 12:1-4).

Notice that after the Lord told Abram (Abraham) to leave, He gave him no more information than that. He didn't know where he was going but he left, knowing that God would lead him to the right place. Yikes! That's faith, wouldn't you say? If that were you, people today would call you crazy. When you tell your wife, children, and father, "Come on, let's go," and they ask, "Where are we going?" and you respond, "I don't know, but God will get us there"—well, they will probably call you crazy too! I question myself if I would not have questioned my husband's stability if he said that to me.

Abraham is known to have made bad decisions before and even lied or told a half-truth, so how could his wife trust him now? He was willing to give his wife to another man to save his own life (see Genesis 12:10-20). That is human thinking, speaking, and seeing as things are now. When you read about Abraham, notice how God referred to him.

Within the story, we see all the flaws and weaknesses of Abraham. We see his humanity when he was scared, weak in his faith, when he lied, in his lack of obedience, and when he had to be told nine times by God about the covenant God was making with him. God did not look at his failings and often defended him, even when I think it was a good time for a teaching moment of correction. God defended Abraham and called him a prophet.

God continually saw Abraham as the finished product, not where he was at that moment. God called him the father of faith. What!? Although Abraham made bad decisions, when he thought about God, he was fully convinced that He was able to accomplish and would do as He promised. Read Romans 4:16-22 and keep that in mind when you read it for yourself:

> *So **the promise is received by faith**. It is given as a free gift. And we are all certain to receive it, whether or not we live according to the law of Moses, if we have **faith like Abraham's**. For Abraham is the father of all who believe. That is what the Scriptures mean when God told him, "I have made you the father of many nations." This happened because **Abraham believed** in the God who brings the dead back to life and who creates new things out of nothing. Even when there was no reason for hope, **Abraham kept hoping**—believing that he would become the father of many nations. For God had said to him, "That's how many descendants you will have!" And Abraham's faith did not weaken, even though,*

at about 100 years of age, he figured his body was as good as dead—and so was Sarah's womb. **Abraham never wavered in believing God's promise.** *In fact, his faith grew stronger, and in this he brought glory to God. He was fully convinced that God is able to do whatever he promises. And* **because of Abraham's faith, God counted him as righteous.**

There were several times when Abraham focused on his ability and knew he was lacking; but when it came to God, he was fully convinced that He was able to do all He said. Abraham's trouble came when He took his focus off God and looked at himself and his ability.

Walking by the flesh and your own strength will always produce fear, so a lesson to learn here is to keep your eyes on God. No thinking, doubting, or listening to others—hold fast to what He said and walk forward. Confusing as it may sound, you can train yourself to do it. Everyone who is saved is given a measure of faith. *"For I say, through the grace given unto me, to every man that is among you, not to think of himself more highly than he ought to think; but to think soberly, according as God hath dealt to every man the measure of faith"* (Romans 12:3 KJV).

Believe it or not that faith resides in your spirit if you have accepted Jesus as your Lord and Savior. The rest is up to you to develop and grow that faith. You get to decide how fast that faith grows. We can learn how to do that in Romans 10:17: *"So faith comes from hearing, that is, hearing the Good News about Christ."*

Hebrews 10:38a (NKJV) says, *"Now the just shall live by faith."* God has given us this faith to strengthen and support us in this life. Matthew 17:20 reads, *"I tell you the truth, if you had faith even as small as a mustard seed, you could say to this mountain, 'Move from here to there,' and it would move. Nothing would be impossible."* Although your faith may be the size of a mustard seed, it still is enough and enables you to do mighty things.

That small measure of faith you received is enough to do whatever He calls you to do. And Jesus is the Author and Finisher of it.

You are born of God, and He is a God of faith. You are His child, and so you are a faith being. God does not do anything outside of faith. As a child of God, you are to live the same way. Hebrews 11:6 (KJV) says, *"But without faith it is impossible to please him: for he that cometh to God must believe that he is, and that he is a rewarder of them that diligently seek him."*

When you plant a flower seed, you have to water it for it to grow. The same is with faith; it does not grow by you forcing it and exclaiming, "I will have faith!" No, because you will eventually fall to the loudest voice in your head that says you are not a person of faith, rather you are a person of failure over and over again. That is you focusing on you and your ability. That is what Abraham did from time to time.

When you are a believer, it is not about you and what you can do—it's about what Jesus already did for you. So if you take what little faith you have and keep watering it with the Word of God, your faith will grow. In 2 Timothy 2:15 we read we need to divide the word of truth rightly: *"Work hard so you can present yourself to God and receive his approval. Be a good worker, one who does not need to be ashamed and who correctly explains the word of truth."* The same verse in the New King James Version states, *"Be diligent to present yourself approved to God, a worker who does not need to be ashamed, rightly dividing the word of truth."*

OK, but what is the word of truth? How do I know it is the word of truth? The Bible is the word of truth! Read it, study it, and you will never be ashamed. No one can trick you with other philosophies if you know it and have it in your heart. You will know it, and the spirit will help you discern it. The more you stay in the Word of God, you will have trained your spirit so much that as soon as someone tries to tell you anything outside of the true gospel your spirit will immediately say no. The truth of your experience cannot be changed, but the truth can change you. As you stay in the Word you will learn God's character, His will, how He thinks, His promises, and suddenly, you will be full of faith, and fully persuaded. First Corinthians 2:14 says, *"But people who aren't spiritual can't receive these truths from God's Spirit. It all sounds foolish to them and they can't understand it, for only those who are spiritual can understand what the Spirit means."*

Build up faith with confession, meditation, and prayer, and you will discover that faith is one of the things that not only pleases God but is vital in every area of your life. We need faith to be saved, to be bold going before the Lord in times of need, to understand how to walk in divine health and prosperity, and to have peace and victory in our lives—we even need faith to die. Right?

Many people wait for the moment before death to believe, but do not be one of them. Tomorrow is promised to no one, so live today as if today would possibly be your last. As you know the time is approaching to die, you need to have faith that everything that God said is true, we begin and end the same way: being fully persuaded that God is, and His Word and promises are true at the beginning and ending of our walk on this earth. We come back to the same Scripture in Hebrews 11:1: *"Faith shows the reality of what we hope for; it is the evidence of things we cannot see."*

I enjoy filling my house with aroma. I find it relaxing and soothing. I was watching my wax melting pot one day, heating it after it cooled off. I watched the wax heat up, and as it melted a bubble began to form in the middle; and then slowly the wax melts from the inside out until the wax is completely melted and hot. As it began to melt, I could smell the aroma very faintly. Not until the wax melted completely does the aroma fill the room. I think about faith that way.

When you start reading God's Word—whether you understand it fully or not—there is life in it, and that life brings a sweet aroma. As you begin in the Word, you don't know how faith grows or the heart changes. Not everything makes sense, and you are not even sure that it is helping or doing what people say it will. But I assure you that if you stay in the Word and continue to read it, something will happen without you even noticing it. Faith starts to bubble up in the center of your heart, and as you stay in the Word, your heart slowly changes until it is entirely soft, washing away all the hardness.

And then you stop one day and look back and see how reading God's Word changed you, and you are different and feel differently. Things such as bad habits are gone and you didn't even realize it. Your heart feels more love and compassion, you are not getting upset at simple things as before, and when you take the time to think about it, you know that His Word has influenced your life in many positive ways.

The Word is a life-giving, soul-cleansing, spiritually healing power that is unexplainable. Confidence is building up in you, and you didn't realize it right away. Fear and shame are not as intense in you. When you smile, your eyes light up with genuine joy. Your soul is not so downcast—now there is new hope, and the future does not look so dismal.

Hebrews 4:12 says, *"For the word of God is alive and powerful. It is sharper than the sharpest two-edged sword, cutting between soul and spirit, between joint and marrow. It exposes our innermost thoughts and desires."*

The Word is heating up, burning away, and refining you from the inside out. It starts inside until it shines through to the outside. So stay the course, and it will be.

Chapter 6

Heart Revelation

Faith is the activator to hope. Hope has no substance, but faith does: *"Now faith is the substance of things hoped for, the evidence of things not seen"* (Hebrews 11:1 KJV). If you have faith in God, you must have faith in His Word. One doesn't come without the other. Faith is acting on the Word. That is when you know God's Word is true. When you reap a harvest from it, that is giving substance to hope.

"I hope so" doesn't move God, but faith moves Him. You can say, "Well, I sure hope God will answer my prayer." That hope will not produce an answer to prayer. But if you say, "Thank You, Lord, I know my prayer is yes and amen because it aligns with Your perfect will for me," that is faith! Faith gets prayers answered. It is confidence in the things we hope.

There is a difference between mentally agreeing with the Word and heart faith. We can relate to that because we were raised to follow our senses. If I can see, feel, hear, and touch it, I will believe. Some people agree with the Word in their human logic, but there is no faith mixed with it, or what I call heart revelation. Mentally agreeing with the Bible is not faith. It can look like faith, but most people cannot tell the difference.

MENTAL ASSENT

Mental assent is agreeing with God's Word as good thoughts or statements. People think, "Yes, that I can agree with." But as soon as there is a real issue in life, they do not believe that the Word of God can be applied to it. It's all surface, fleshy, natural belief. There is no impact or transformation where it goes from the ears and head down to the heart for change to take effect. They agree with God, but do not believe in Him.

What I am talking about is heart faith, not mental assent. God is not asking you if you agree with what He is saying or if you know a better way. The mental agreement means you agree to what is said, but it doesn't go any farther than your head: "Yes, yes, I know that is what it says…but!" As soon as you say, "but," that cancels out everything that was said before. Do not try to logically concur with something the Word of God means, believe that what He is saying to you is true.

I experienced a student with that mentality as I was teaching one of my classes on faith. There was a young couple who seemed overly confident in themselves and made it known that they were going to show it to the class and me. They sat in the front row closest to me.

From the moment I began the course, the husband kept interrupting me. At first, I let patience overrule my instinct of telling him how rude he was being. With every interjection, his wife smiled and concurred with his thought process, saying, "That's right," or, "Yes, honey." He was counteracting every word I said from the Bible and course outline, saying that faith was all in the mind. The power was in the mind.

He ultimately tried to take over the class and said, "Listen, I have learned from so-and-so on YouTube, and I recommend you watch what he has to say too." He was stating that if you think about it long enough and put all your focus on what you want and then keep saying it, you will have it. It has nothing to do with Jesus; rather, it has everything to do with you, your will, and how you think. That was it!

Other students were correcting him, and now anger rose up in me, and I responded to him with Scripture, stating this is not about mental assent—it is about *faith, heart revelation, and the Word* coming alive in you.

The husband and his wife smugly smiled as I rendered my explanation of the truth. With all that was in me, I wanted to toss him from the class. The wife then recoiled and tried to backtrack, "Oh nooo, he thinks Jesus is good and all…" I cut her off and did not allow them to speak another word: "This class is not your opportunity to proclaim your sales pitch."

After class, I went to the director of this particular campus who is also the pastor of the church. As soon as I mentioned his name, the pastor interjected and said, "Oh YES, what a gifted man of God. I'm going to have him in leadership, he is clearly called of God." I quietly, with a surprised look on my face said, "I was going to say he needs some guidance and counseling, particularly on the Scriptures, he lacks real understanding of God's Word."

The pastor looked surprised; but within me, I knew there was no use continuing the conversation. As the next week came along, I prayed about the situation and talked with the Lord about it. I went to class determined not to tolerate any interruptions again in my classroom. If they interrupted once, they were going to be asked to leave the class and never return. The class was not about them and their pitch from some self-proclaimed apostle of God to go against the true Word of God. I had a classroom full of students who wanted accurate teachings and that is what I was going to present.

Guess what? The husband never came back to class. The rumor going around was that he was saying, "How does this woman think she knows anything and can teach me anything?" The wife returned for one more class and tried to be as attentive as possible with agreeing at every step. Except she missed the point. My mistake was even to allow him to interrupt more than once.

The unfortunate rest of the story is that the pastor did place him and his wife in a top leadership position of the church after being new members for only a short time. I'm not aware of the whole story, but it did not end well.

Please understand that it is not faith; God is all about heart. Everything comes back to the heart. You cannot wish so hard in your head to go to Heaven; you will not get there if you do. You can wish for God to love you. But you do not have to wish for it, He already does.

Romans 10:10 (NIV) clearly states it is with your heart that you believe, not your mind: *"For **it is with your heart** that you believe and are justified, and it is with your mouth that you profess your faith and are saved."* Mark 11:23 also says that we must believe in our heart: *"I tell you the truth, you can say to this mountain, 'May you be lifted up and thrown into the sea,'* *and it will happen. But you must really believe it will happen and have no doubt in your heart."*

Some people say, "I *know* God's Word is true!" That is head knowledge, not heart revelation. It's about heart faith, not mind faith, or what I call a natural faith. You can go to the light switch and flip it up so that it will turn on and you have faith, that is natural human faith.

I am talking about *heart faith* that goes beyond your mind, will, and emotions. With heart faith, you can believe in your heart and still doubt in your head. Your mind can talk you out of most anything. With natural faith, you are also relying on yourself with a works mentality. It has nothing to do with Jesus or what He has done for you. The mind is mighty; just not what it takes to come to salvation. It will not transform you.

James 1:22 says, *"But don't just listen to God's word. You must do what it says. Otherwise, you are only fooling yourselves."*

Even for myself, if I read the Scriptures, I can say, "Yes, I believe that!" Except I stop and think, "Is that me mentally agreeing or do **I believe**?": Believing is not as easy as people proclaim. You may never know if you really believe until you are faced with a situation: Do you *believe* God for the answer to work it out, or do you fall into depression and hopelessness? Do you have a situation arise in your life and look up to the Lord and say, "Here You go, Lord, this is Your problem now. I know You can handle it better than I can"? Do you then let go of the stress of it to Him? Or do you say, "Now what do I do? How can I solve this situation?" I test myself to see if I genuinely believe.

Here are three things to consider when testing your belief system:

1. Heart faith says, I have it!
2. The world faith says, I believe it when I see it!
3. But true faith says, I believe it before seeing it!

How about doubting Thomas and faithful Abraham?

Thomas, one of Jesus's disciples, was a skeptic who refused to believe Jesus had visited all the other ten apostles upon His resurrection unless he could feel the nail holes in Jesus's hands or place his hand in His side. He would believe *if!* So Jesus told Thomas to come, touch, feel. Then He said to him, *"Don't be faithless any longer. Believe!"* (John 20:27c). Then Thomas believed. This is where the phrase "Doubting Thomas" came from.

Thomas was not all bad; he was loyal and asked some of the tough questions. For example, John 14:5-6 says, *"'No, we don't know, Lord,' Thomas said. 'We have no idea where you are going, so how can we know the way?' Jesus told him, 'I am the way, the truth, and the life. No one can come to the Father except through me.'"*

I can say I am guilty of that. There are times in my life when situations came up, and my faith wasn't trusting in Jesus but doubting on whether or not He would help or come through unless He gave me a sign.

Read Romans 4:1b-3 about the faith of Abraham:

> *What did he discover about being made right with God? If his good deeds had made him acceptable to God, he would have had something to boast about. But that was not God's way. For the Scriptures tell us, "Abraham*

*believed God, and God counted him as **righteous because of his faith.**"*

When hope seemed gone, Abraham continued to believe God. He never wavered in God's promises. Abraham wavered in his ability to accomplish things, but when it came to God, he never hesitated. He was convinced of God's ability. Let's consider Mark 11:22-24 (AMP):

> *Jesus replied, "Have faith in God [constantly]. I assure you and most solemnly say to you, whoever says to this mountain, 'Be lifted up and thrown into the sea!' and does not doubt in his heart [in God's unlimited power], but believes that what he says is going to take place, it will be done for him [in accordance with God's will]. For this reason I am telling you, whatever things you ask for in prayer [in accordance with God's will], believe [with confident trust] that you have received them, and they will be given to you".*

Don't try to believe with your mind or physically try—believe it in your heart. This is true with every area of your spiritual life. It's all heart. Don't try—do it or don't. If you say I will "try" to the Word, you can stop right there because I can already tell you are not going to receive any answers. Try means to make an attempt or effort to do something. I will give it a try and see if it works—that is a doubting Thomas syndrome. Faith is believing; faith believes without seeing.

WHAT ABOUT FEELINGS?

Feelings have nothing to do with faith. Feelings come and go, and our emotions should not lead us. On my worse days when I felt no presence of God, the best things happened when I prayed either for myself or someone else. It had nothing to do with my feelings. The order should be God's Word first, then feelings. Not the reverse.

Faith is now! It is active in the present and future. Faith is not past tense. When you believe for something, hold on to your faith until you have it. If you have something you no longer have to have the faith to receive it, you have it!

Don't say, "When I'm healed I will believe Jesus healed me." NO! Believe God's Word that says you *are* healed (Isaiah 53:5 NKJV). Say, "By His stripes I am healed!" And then you receive. Take out your mind and emotions and focus on the Word and what Jesus did for you.

I know plenty of people who ran to the altar call wailing, screaming, and then jumping for joy hugging everyone and in reality, they did not get saved. I have also seen people go to the altar with no emotion at all, say the prayer, and then turn around and go back to their seat. People stared as he went by and murmured, "Aww, poor thing, he didn't get saved." But in reality, he did get saved and his life was transformed. He left the church, went home, and his whole life was changed in that instant. Don't be deceived by emotions or fleshly acts; it's all about heart and the change internally.

If you don't know this already—you are a triune being, meaning you are body, soul, and spirit. When I speak of believing with your heart, I am not talking about the heart pumping within your chest. I am talking about you, your spirit. Your spirit, which you are, has a heart. You have a body that you need to live in this world, but the real you is a spirit.

Knowing that should help you understand that Romans 10:10 and Mark 11:23 a little better. *You believe with your spiritual heart.*

That realization pertains to salvation, too. You believed and were saved. You believed with your spirit heart, not your mind or the heart organ. The spirit of a person is the heart of the person. Jesus said in John 4:24, *"For God is Spirit, so those who worship him must worship in spirit and in truth."* Moreover, John 3:6 (MSG) says,

> *Jesus said, "You're not listening. Let me say it again. Unless a person submits to this original creation—the 'wind-hovering-over-the-water' creation, the invisible moving the visible, a baptism into a new life—it's not possible to enter God's kingdom. When you look at a baby, it's just that: a body you can look at and touch. But the person who takes shape within is formed by something you can't see and touch—the Spirit—and becomes a living spirit".*

Everyone is made up of three parts: spirit, soul, and body. You can see this in 1 Thessalonians 5:23: *"Now may the God of peace make you holy in every way, and may your whole spirit and soul and body be kept blameless until our Lord Jesus Christ comes again."* You live in a body, your soul made up of your mind, will, and emotions, and then you have a spirit. You worship the Lord spirit to Spirit, not in your mind.

You can relate this to renewing your mind as well. When you were saved, it was your spirit that was reborn, not your body or mind. Otherwise, why is Paul telling the Roman Christians to renew their minds and present their bodies? Second Corinthians 5 talks about our bodies being our house. So as we live in this house while here on earth, we are not present with the Lord, but once our bodies die, we will be present with the Lord. Consider 2 Corinthians 5:1-10:

> *For we know that when this earthly tent we live in is taken down (that is, when we die and leave this earthly body), we will have a house in heaven, an eternal body made for us by God himself and not by human hands. We grow weary in our present bodies, and we long to put on our heavenly bodies like new clothing. For we will put on heavenly bodies; we will not be spirits without bodies. While we live in these earthly bodies, we groan and sigh, but it's not that we want to die and get rid of these bodies that clothe us. Rather, we want to put on our new bodies so that these dying bodies will be swallowed up by life. God himself has prepared us for this, and as a guarantee he has given us his Holy Spirit. So we are always confident, even though we know that as long as we live in these bodies we are not at home with the Lord. For we live by believing and not by seeing. Yes, we are fully confident, and we would rather be away from these earthly bodies, for then we will be at home with the Lord. So whether we are here in this body or away from this body, our goal is to please him. For we must all stand before Christ to be judged. We will each receive whatever we deserve for the good or evil we have done in this earthly body.*

This truth is also written about in 1 Peter 3:4: *"You should **clothe yourselves** instead **with the beauty that comes from within**, the unfading beauty of a gentle and quiet spirit, which is so precious to God."*

This is how revelation comes too. The more you fill your heart, your spiritual heart, with the Word of God, God brings revelation; and suddenly, after reading the same Scripture 500 times, meaning comes to your inner self! Sometimes, in fact the majority of the time, people listening to a service are listening with their minds and not their hearts. Quiet your mind and train it to listen with your hidden heart. You will be amazed at how much you will learn and understand.

Proverbs 3:5 says, *"Trust in the LORD with all your heart; do not depend on your own understanding."*

Leaning unto your own understanding is talking about your mind. That's why you must cast down every imagination that exalts itself above the Word of God hidden in your heart. Second Corinthians 10:4-5 reads, *"We use God's mighty weapons, not worldly weapons, to knock down the strongholds of human reasoning and to destroy false arguments. We destroy every proud obstacle that keeps people from knowing God. We capture their rebellious thoughts and teach them to obey Christ."*

Eventually, we will be walking by the Word and faith and not by our natural eyes and feelings. We then enter into rest: *"For only we who believe can enter his rest. As for the others, God said, 'In my anger I took an oath: "They will never enter my place of rest,"' even though this rest has been ready since he made the world"* (Hebrews 4:3).

Is it making more sense now? When you take your mind out of a situation, take feelings out, and what you see with your natural eyes, and walk by what God says, there is no anxiety, worry, or fret!

IMPERFECT BUT DESPERATE FAITH

Jesus got into the boat again and went back to the other side of the lake, where a large crowd gathered around him on the shore. Then a leader of the local synagogue, whose name was Jairus, arrived. When he saw Jesus, he fell at his feet, pleading fervently with him. "My little daughter is dying," he said. "Please come and lay your hands on her; heal her so she can live." Jesus went with him, and all the people followed, crowding around him. A woman in the crowd had suffered for twelve years with constant bleeding. She had suffered a great deal from many doctors, and over the years she had spent everything she had to pay them, but she had gotten no better. In fact, she had gotten worse. She had heard about Jesus, so she came up behind him through the crowd and touched his robe. For she thought to herself, "If I can just touch his robe, I will be healed." Immediately the bleeding stopped, and she could feel in her body that she had been healed of her terrible condition. Jesus realized at once that healing power had gone out from him, so he turned around in the crowd and asked, "Who touched my robe?" His disciples said to him, "Look at this crowd pressing around you. How can you ask, 'Who touched me?'" But he kept on looking around to see who had done it. Then the frightened woman, trembling at the realization of what had happened to her, came and fell to her knees in front of him and told him what she had done. And he said to her, "Daughter, your faith has made you well. Go in peace. Your suffering is over."

—Mark 5:21-34

This woman had been beaten down and was feeling hopeless. She was probably wearing rags because she gave everything to try to be healed by the practicing doctors at that time. Never getting better, she is now frail, poverty-stricken, and desperate. Then one day she hears of this man named Jesus and how He goes about healing people. Having nothing left, her imperfect faith thought, "If I could crawl up through the crowd and touch even the hem of His garment, I will be healed. Then I can shrink back and go my way and no one will be the wiser."

Everyone was pushing on Him, demanding for something from Him anyway. Who is she compared to the religious leader's daughter? The religious leader's daughter would be more important than she. Would He even consider healing her if she approached him? The woman suffering from constant bleeding seems to be a little selfish. She wasn't thinking of Jesus or anyone else only that she wanted to be cured of this disease.

Her pure, imperfect, and desperate faith pulled healing directly from His clothes, sucking out the anointing. Now remember, Jesus didn't know or stop to heal her; this is all her effort. Imperfect, uneducated scripturally, and attending church without anything to give brings a whole other dynamic of shame and unworthiness—yet Jesus felt her pull and stopped.

This woman thought she could touch the bottom of Jesus's garment, be healed, and then slink away. But now she is trembling with fear at being noticed. Now she fears for her life. Not only was this woman forbidden to be out in public by law, she went into a crowd of people, touching many people as she tried to reach Jesus. Now Jesus Himself knows anointing left Him. So He abruptly stops and asks who touched Him.

Terrified, she fell at His feet, and admitted she was the one who touched Him. Can you hear the gasps of people as she told her story? And this woman touched many of them as well. But she knew she was healed, and so her punishment was acceptable. As soon as she touched the hem of His garment, the bleeding stopped.

I suggest that the woman no longer looked frail or sickly. Once she touched His garment, healing filled her body, she felt stronger, and a healthy glow came upon her face. So when Jesus questioned who did it and she confessed, people stared at her. But I dare say, she didn't look ill any longer.

Then, what did Jesus do? He didn't scold her; instead, He said, *"Daughter, your faith has made you well. Go in peace. Your suffering is over."*

As I pondered on this story, I learned three things this woman did on faith:

1. She heard.
2. She believed.
3. She acted.

As with anything in this life, there can be hindrances or interferences of faith. It is never easy to take a look at ourselves, except if you are praying and not receiving answers it would be beneficial to you to stop and take inventory. Taking inventory from time to time is to examine yourself to see whether you are in the faith. The woman with the issue of blood heard, believed, and then acted. Commonly people say they are walking by faith but are speaking words that are contrary to faith. It is good to step back from time to time and see where we are in our walk with God.

Here are a few truths from God's Word to remember:

Faith does not work in an unforgiving heart: *"But when you are praying, first forgive anyone you are holding a grudge against, so that your Father in heaven will forgive your sins, too"* (Mark 11:25).

Faith works by love: *"For when we place our faith in Christ Jesus, there is no benefit in being circumcised or being uncircumcised. What is important is faith expressing itself in love"* (Galatians 5:6).

Faith and love are connected. They depend on each other. Why? Most people know the chapter of love as 1 Corinthians 13. Let's read a portion of it (1 Corinthians 13:1-3):

> *If I could speak all the languages of earth and of angels, but didn't love others, I would only be a noisy gong or a clanging cymbal. If I had the gift of prophecy, and if I understood all of God's secret plans and possessed all knowledge, and if I had such faith that I could move mountains, but didn't love others, I would be nothing. If I gave everything I have to the poor and even sacrificed my body, I could boast about it; but if I didn't love others, I would have gained nothing.*

Read a little further in 1 Corinthians 13:7-8a (AMPC):

> *Love bears up under anything and everything that comes, is ever ready to believe the best of every person, its hopes are fadeless under all circumstances, and it endures everything [without weakening]. Love never fails [never fades out or becomes obsolete or comes to an end].*

Everything is connected. You can't walk in faith without love, and you can't walk in love without faith. We are commanded to love: *"So now I am giving you a new commandment: Love each other. Just as I have loved you, you should love each other"* (John 13:34).

Conclusion: Never get out of love.

There is one more hindrance—the **lack of understanding**: *"My people are destroyed for lack of knowledge"* (Hosea 4:6a KJV).

After coming to salvation, you need to renew your mind and get understanding. Learn who you now are in Christ. If you struggle with that, find someone to help you learn how to do that. Concerning renewing, apostle Paul said in 2 Corinthians 5:17, *"This means that anyone who belongs to Christ has become a new person. The old life is gone; a new life has begun!"*

HOW CAN WE BUILD OUR FAITH?

Proverbs 4:20-22 tell us how we can build our faith: *"My child, pay attention to what I say. Listen carefully to my words. Don't lose sight of them. Let them penetrate deep into your heart, for they bring life to those who find them, and healing to their whole body."*

Chapter 7

Forgiveness

Make allowance for each other's faults, and forgive anyone who offends you. Remember, the Lord forgave you, so you must forgive others.
—Colossians 3:13

In my early Christian days, some people would say and do things to me, and then later in front of other people they denied it. Not only was it hurtful, it also angered me because people would believe them and they would get away with it and not be held accountable. So in anger, I decided to put things in writing and hold on to pictures, emails, voice messages, or anything that would prove I was telling the truth, and that they were lying. Basically, I was keeping a log of their wrongs and would use the evidence to throw it in their faces before everyone when they would deny it.

At this time, I was in lay ministry at church, and my responsibility was to keep in contact with the people assigned to me in my area. Weekly, I would meet up with them or give them a call and pray for them if there were any needs; later I would complete a report to the district pastor. In this way, the church was able to touch all the members.

This one particular night, I was at my desk and reading the Bible and gathering Scriptures before I began calling people to pray and minister to them. While I was reading, the Lord said, "I want to talk to you about something." He said, "I want you to quit holding records of wrong against people." My heart sunk, and I saw a picture of my actions. I didn't think of it that way. It was a way for me to be justified. He said, "I didn't create you to handle that, give it to Me. I will remember what they have done to you and take care of it when the time comes. You are not to take care of it. Vengeance doesn't belong to you." By the time He was finished talking to me, I was in tears.

I responded, "But God, they do this and that repeatedly! I am tired of it!" He said nothing in response. Rather, He said, "Now before you go on, call so-and-so and tell her you forgive her." WHAT? Fear gripped me. The last thing I wanted to do was call and tell this person I forgave her.

I responded, "Lord, she is going to think I'm crazy!" He said no more.

It took me some time to gather my strength and get my emotions in line before calling her. Out of obedience, I picked up the phone, called this woman, and told her why I was upset at her. I confessed my grudge and said that the Lord told me to call her and forgive her. In tears I said, "So I want you to know that I forgive you." As soon as I did that, something broke inside me and I felt free. There is no way to really explain it other than that.

On the other end of the phone, I heard her laugh and tell her husband that I called to say I forgive her and the Lord told me to do it. And just as I imagined, she thought I was crazy. I ended the call saying, "Well, I just wanted to tell you that. Have a good day," and we ended the call. My willingness and obedience, despite my feelings, set me free.

Notice what God didn't do—He never talked to me about this woman's trespass against me; He dealt with my issues. Feeling the freedom, it didn't matter anymore if she received my forgiveness or not. That was not God's intention. He was correcting and teaching me so I could go on to do the things He needed me to do. I let go of holding any list of other people's wrongs, including this woman, from that moment forward. That night of calling people assigned to me was one of my best nights of ministry and prayer.

You may be wondering, "Why is she writing about forgiving that woman and not forgiving her father?" That may seem more natural than forgiving my father, my abuser. To me, it is the same in many ways. No one would blame me in this world if I dragged him through the mud and held on to hatred toward him—and all men for that matter. I could keep the list of evils he had done, but what good is that for me? The one getting sick from it all is me, not my dad.

When you forgive someone, it is for your best interest and healing. Once I learned to let go and genuinely forgive someone who wronged me, then God could deal with that person.

If I insist on holding on to the wrongs, they are imprisoning me. Forgiveness is not condoning the behavior, nor is it ignoring the horror and anger of the situation. But if I continue to live like a victim and excuse all of my bad behavior because of my wounds, then I am not healed. I am still being victimized.

Forgiveness comes from facing the hard truths, anger, and pain from the abuse. He did not get away with anything. The Lord helped me through the grief of all of it. It wasn't instant. It took years for me to allow Him to help me through it, and perhaps there is more, but He will deal with it in the proper time. The Lord allowed me to feel the pain, cry, feel sorry for myself, and be angry. Once I went through one issue, He took me through the next issue; and after all that, He still did not reject me and then acceptance, release, and healing came.

Feeling anger is not a sin. As long as there is more than one person on the planet, someone is going to get angry. The Scripture says, *"Be angry, and do not sin"* (Ephesians 4:26a NKJV). It means you can and will get angry but do not let your anger control you. Letting the anger control you is the sin. Sometimes we have to vent, and once that is released, then we can listen. Jesus is understanding of our needs as human beings. When we feel like we are not heard, that is when we keep yelling all the louder. It is natural human nature to want to be heard, understood, and affirmed.

Jesus did that for me. He is our Counselor. Jesus is the Counselor like no other. Isaiah 9:6 calls Him a "Wonderful Counselor." The counselors of the world can give good advice or bad advice; with Jesus, it is the ultimate best advice. His advice is timely and accurate. He can help us if we allow Him.

ABSOLUTE FORGIVENESS

Part of forgiveness is to forgive those who have violated you in any way, major or minor. Another part is to forgive those who were supposed to help you and didn't. For example, if you were raped or molested and you tried to tell someone, reach out for help, and it was ignored or went unheard, you can easily hold unforgiveness against that person. A significant part of your relationship with Jesus is to forgive those people. "I can't!" you might say. Or, "How could they not help me? Why wouldn't they do something?" Please know when you pray those prayers, some of those questions will never be answered, and sometimes they will. The answers you do not receive will be the ones you need to give to the Lord, trusting you may never have those answers in this life.

Let it go and forgive them. I learned that it was almost always fear on the other person's part that kept them from helping me. You may have been abused, but they may have been abused as well, even by the same person. So they walk in fear of what might happen to them; or they don't know how to rescue themselves from the situation, let alone rescue you. They snap at you because their thoughts are consumed with how to get themselves out of the situation or even protect themselves. Remember, violator/abusers are controllers and manipulators, and their biggest weapon is fear. It's human nature to self-preserve.

For myself, I tried several times to ask for help. Telling people I trusted enough to risk the shame; and I even begged, cried, and pleaded for help. I was asking to be rescued. The responses I received were a slap in the face, being threatened, and a flat-out no. That only added to my pain, shame, feeling of hopelessness, and despair. No one loved me enough to help me, fight for me, or rescue me? It must be true. I am worthless and unlovable. Turning inside and setting up a wall was the only way I knew to protect myself from any more hurt.

My self-preservation clicked in, and I became withdrawn. There wasn't any meanness in me; my behavior was still obedient, kind, and helpful. When I talked, I was soft spoken, and always with an undertone of self-doubt.

As time went on and I grew in my spiritual maturity, the Lord helped me to see and understand those people differently. I know now that they were just as afraid as I was of the abuser. It wasn't abnormal to be beaten in our home, punished with no food, or forbidden to associate with other family members. If I was treated that way, others in the same environment were treated the same. They lived in the paralyzing fear that I did.

My mother, after working three jobs, came home and was more often than not, beaten by her husband. She did nothing to deserve that. It didn't take much for him to get angry with her, sometimes it was just a word she said or didn't say, or no reason at all. Today, when I think about it, I am surprised at how we cowered to the fear of one person in the family when there were more of us than one of him. Yet we all cowered, afraid of him. That is the power of fear!

As the Lord worked on healing me, I began to understand the people who didn't rescue me. They didn't hate me; they lived in the same torment and felt trapped just like me. They wanted to be free but didn't know the answer either. My heart began to ache for them. Instead of hate, I cried and prayed for them. I would ask the Lord to heal them of their wounds as I was being healed. I prayed that the Lord would help them to see that they are no longer captives—that He would break all the shackles off them so they could walk a free life, filled with love and peace in their hearts.

Have you heard the phrase, "Hurt people hurt people"? This is true. Or have you heard, "They will never change, they are just angry, bitter people"? That is not true in my estimation. I am a firm believer that Jesus loves, and His love can do what we think is impossible. I've witnessed several individuals, men and women, change from being angry, bitter to soft and tenderhearted people.

Unless you can reach out for that love or have someone help you, the reality is you will stay in bondage. The fear, shame, humiliation, and despair place blinders on your eyes to where you cannot see the truth. Jesus removes those blinders. There is a tomorrow, and it can be more wonderful than you ever imagined. Forget about what you believe and think. Do not lean to your understanding. It's distorted. Proverbs 3:5 says, *"Trust in the LORD with all your heart; do not depend on your own understanding."*

For many years, my life was filled with guilt and shame; I believed it was hopeless and that not even God could love someone like me.

Fear is a liar! Fear is all just smoke and mirrors. The strength to take the step doesn't take much—just ask, believe, and walk forward. The rest of the toil is His! If you can focus on learning who you are in Jesus Christ, the rest will work itself out; six months later, you will see a difference. Then twelve months later and every year after that, you will look back and see a transformation you didn't think possible.

Forgiveness is not easy because we think we have to *feel* like forgiving them. We think, "Until I can fell like it, I won't forgive." The truth is, forgiveness has nothing to do with emotion. Forgiveness is a decision.

The good news is you can forgive people, and the Bible has many Scriptures regarding the necessity of forgiveness. The only person carrying the burden of unforgiveness is you, not the other person. Even if they are carrying the burden, you are not responsible for their issues; you are responsible for yours. Let us consider the following Scriptures urging us to forgive others: *"Get rid of all bitterness, rage, anger, harsh words, and slander, as well as all types of evil behavior. Instead, be kind to each other, tenderhearted, forgiving one another, just as God through Christ has forgiven you"* (Ephesians 4:31-32). *"But when you are praying, first forgive anyone you are holding a grudge against, so that your Father in heaven will forgive your sins, too"* (Mark 11:25). *"Make allowance for each other's faults, and forgive anyone who offends you. Remember, the Lord forgave you, so you must forgive others"* (Colossians 3:13). *"And forgive us our sins, as we have forgiven those who sin against us"* (Matthew 6:12).

There is a power beyond understanding in walking in continual forgiveness. At first, it will take all of your strength to utter even a couple of words of blessing regarding the person(s). Take baby steps and start by saying a small, simple prayer, asking God to please bless so-and-so in Jesus's name, amen. That may seem like I asked you to move Mount Everest. Still, do it. In doing this small step, you begin to allow Jesus access to help you.

When you are stronger, allow the Holy Spirit to help you find Scripture and pray over them. Keep building up your prayers and blessings, and I promise if your heart is sincere, you will come to a day when you can say hello, hug, and tell those people you love them and mean it: *"For I can do everything through Christ, who gives me strength"* (Philippians 4:13).

We can believe we have forgiven them, but the real test is always when you see them and all the feelings come flooding back, and we begin to growl inside. Those are only emotions. Stop it! Refuse it. Don't say you can't, because I am a testimony that you can. We are not different. Nothing is being recommended or encouraged here that I did not have to go through myself. After being beaten, raped, abandoned, left as an outcast with no one in my life, I had every right to be angry, mean, and feel as if the world owed me something. That is all true if my emotions ruled me. Instead, I chose God's way.

Jesus is an excellent example of forgiveness. Even on the cross, Jesus said, "Father, forgive them": *"Jesus said, 'Father, forgive them, for they don't know what they are doing'"* (Luke 23:34a).

If people could step outside of themselves and see with clear eyesight, they would not do what they are doing. Unfortunately, most will not see it until they leave this life. Jesus knew this about us. We cannot see our true selves, yet He saw beyond us. His final thoughts of us as He hung on the cross suffering were not of anger or unforgiveness; instead, He prayed for us from His heart, *"Father, forgive them, for they don't know what they are doing."* Can I do any less? Can you do any less? He forgave us, and likewise, we need to forgive those who have sinned against us. When you come to the truth of that, forgiveness is easy.

Chapter 8

Renewing Your Mind

> *Don't copy the behavior and customs of this world, but let God transform you into a new person by changing the way you think. Then you will learn to know God's will for you, which is good and pleasing and perfect.*
>
> —Romans 12:2

Most people today, especially Christians, walk in a continual state of condemnation.

They think that God loves you when you do good things and is angry with you when you do something wrong. Condemnation is a very powerful word. When we condemn homes, what does that mean? That the house is unlivable and unfit for use in this life; it is worthless. That is how most Christians live in a mental state of condemnation before God and other people. They walk in a mental state of worthlessness and feeling unfit for use. They feel they are worthless to God, and that He would not use them in any way. That person is walking in condemnation. If you think the preachers you see on TV have it all together, and that of course God would use them or answer their prayers and not you because you are not as holy as them, you are wrong. They do not have it any more together in life than you and they do not have more favor of Him than you. That is a lie that people have learned, but it is not the way God sees you. Apostle Paul declared in Romans 8:1 (KJV), *"There is therefore now no condemnation to them which are in Christ Jesus, who walk not after the flesh, but after the Spirit. For the law of the Spirit of life in Christ Jesus hath made me free from the law of sin and death."*

Let's read the same scriptural passage in The Message translation:

> *With the arrival of Jesus, the Messiah, that fateful dilemma is resolved. Those who enter into Christ's being-here-for-us no longer have to live under a continuous, low-lying black cloud. A new power is in operation. The Spirit of life in Christ, like a strong wind, has magnificently cleared the air, freeing you from a fated lifetime of brutal tyranny at the hands of sin and death.*

God is not displeased with you or condemning you in any way. If you belong to Jesus, there is no condemnation toward you at all. God is not angry with you. Only under the Law of Moses were we brought to the understanding that we are sinners, and no one is right in God's sight. However, after Jesus, we are all righteous before God because of Jesus. Jesus paid the price of our sinful nature.

You should not have a sin consciousness after accepting Jesus as your Lord and Savior. The author of the book of Hebrews wrote, *"For then would they not have ceased to be offered? because that the worshipers once purged should have had no more conscience of sins"* (Hebrews 10:2 KJV). The New Living Translation renders the same Scripture this way, *"If they could have provided perfect cleansing, the sacrifices would have stopped, for the worshipers would have been purified once for all time, and their feelings of guilt would have disappeared."*

Let's also read Romans 10:4 (KJV): *"For Christ is the end of the law for righteousness to every one that believeth."* And consider Romans 10:4-10 (MSG):

> *The earlier revelation was intended simply to get us ready for the Messiah, who then puts everything right for those who trust him to do it. Moses wrote that anyone who insists on using the law code to live right before God soon discovers it's not so easy—every detail of life regulated by fine print! But trusting God to shape the right living in us is a different story—no precarious climb up to heaven to recruit the Messiah, no dangerous descent into hell to rescue the Messiah. So what exactly was Moses saying? The word that saves is right here, as near as the tongue in your mouth, as close as the heart in your chest. It's the word of faith that welcomes God to go to work and set things right for us. This is the core of our preaching. Say the welcoming word to God—"Jesus is my Master"—embracing, body and soul, God's work of doing in us what he did in raising Jesus from the dead. That's it. You're not "doing" anything; you're simply calling out to God, trusting him to do it for you. That's salvation. With your whole being you embrace God setting things right, and then you say it, right out loud: "God has set everything right between him and me!"*

Replace your sin consciousness with righteous consciousness. Before you accepted Jesus as your Lord and Savior, you lived under the Law of Moses or the Ten Commandments; but after Jesus, you no longer have to work to be right before God, you are already righteous before God, because of Jesus. So let go of your past life and put on your new nature: *"Put on your new nature, created to be like God—truly righteous and holy"* (Ephesians 4:24).

As we grow in the knowledge and understanding of who we are in Jesus without effort, we will grow in confidence. Now, there will be days when you mess up, and you can go right back to tearing yourself down—but don't do it. Practice the things that you have learned about your new nature. Consider 1 John 3:19 (KJV): *"And hereby we know that we are of the truth, and shall assure our hearts before him."* Thus, we need to assure our hearts that we belong to Jesus: *"For if our heart condemn us, God is greater than our heart, and knoweth all things"* (1 John 3:20 KJV).

We may condemn ourselves, but God is not condemning us. Remember, God is greater than our hearts and He knows all things, even better than we know ourselves.

Eventually, as we stay in the Word and our spirit keeps growing, then 1 John 3:21 (KJV) happens: *"Beloved, if our heart condemn us not, then have we confidence toward God."*

That old religious way of thinking will disappear, and God's way of thinking and how you believe He sees you becomes a reality. You have renewed your mind.

HURTFUL LIES AS TRUTH

When I was growing up in the environment of abuse, my mind was utterly petrified with fear. Petrified? That's a pretty strong word. Yes, it is the correct word. Petrified means you are so afraid you are unable to move. My dad had that ability over me. When he looked at me, I froze, even to the point of not wanting to breathe. I was paralyzed by fear. I would stand still and take the beating. I couldn't even utter a word or express tears to cry—until I went to my room away from his presence, closed the door, and then would uncontrollably cry.

Because I lived in a petrified state of fear, it affected my sleep. I never slept as a child because my mind was always fearful of knowing that at any moment he could walk into my room and take me to his room to abuse me.

My dad also played with my mind and that of my siblings, pitting us against each other. He was trying to make us hate and be jealous of each other. It was a sick and depraved mind that taught his daughters to be jealous because he took one of us to his room to be with him. An unknowing, tender mind of a child can be destroyed this way. He told me once that he could not find a good woman on this earth, so he created his own—his daughters.

His thoughts about women were hideous, a recurring living nightmare for my sisters and me. He thought that women were good for cooking, cleaning, sex, and babies. Outside of that, women of any age should be seen and not heard.

As his demented worldview tormented my thoughts, God did something in me even then. Inside, I would hear, "No." I never thought further than that, but my spirit said no. Right then and there my spirit refused that way of looking at life. Yet the living nightmares were recorded and on replay in my mind. God's soft voice echoed through the pain and fear, and somehow I knew there was something different in life. I knew it, except the way to get there was unknown. These voices in my mind would war against each other constantly.

One time, my mom and I were walking home, and one of my mom's so-called best friends stopped to talk to her. In her conversation, she said how terrible and what a shame it was for my mom to be going through such things—being beaten, working so hard, and the way he treated the children. She was saying this even before the whole truth was exposed. She then looked down at me and said, "Oh poor thing, she will either end up to be gay, a hooker, or in prison." My mom stood silently, waiting for her to stop talking so we could go on our way. I dropped my head in shame; but in my spirit, I said, "NOT ME!" What a horrible thing to speak to a friend and in front of her child.

Dearest reader, if you have people in your life like that, know without a doubt that person is not a friend. I remember it still today, and it breaks my heart for my mom. Instead of helping, hugging, praying for her, or being there as a friend and a shoulder to cry on, she ripped my mom to shreds with a soft voice and a smile.

The small Voice that kept echoing through the pain, today I believe that was part of what helped me overcome. God's Spirit in me, quietly but adamantly and continually said, "NO!"

But at that point I didn't know how to allow it to sink in and become real in my spirit. My mind, however, tormented me and brought those things to my remembrance.

All of the voices and tapes would replay in my mind all the time, and they were louder than the soft, internal Voice that counteracted them. For most of my childhood and some of my adulthood, I worked hard not to be what people said. As I read of the women in the Old Testament, it would be my goal to be like them—willing, obedient, humble, chaste—and then I would be acceptable not only to people but most of all to God. Except nothing ever seemed like it was enough, no matter how much I begged, pleaded, and cried.

Thank God for my hunger and passion for striving to know and understand more, and for the first people who came into my life to teach and explain to me the truth of the gospel. The way I was living was not the gospel. Gospel means good news, so how is that good news to me? The real good news transformed me and continually sets me free.

LISTEN TO HIS SOFT, SMALL VOICE

Have you suffered in such a way? Did you take the words spoken over you as truth when you heard them? Is that what you believe today in your heart and mind? The power of the words we speak and the power of the mind and how those words sink into our hearts condemned us and directed our lives because we believed them. Why did you believe them? Because the words came from a person you trusted, admired, or relied on for teaching you the way of life.

They played again and again on constant repeat, and you began to see yourself that way, and believed the words until they went from your head and sank into your heart.

Friend, those hurtful words are what we have to erase from our hearts and minds and renew ourselves with God's lovingkindness. We cannot do it alone, because we do not know how. We only know what we are taught. Those condemning tapes need to be burned. If you continually meditate on those voices and words spoken over you, you are never really moving beyond your past; it is now continually your present.

Even after I was out and away from the situation at home, the words and his actions plagued me. Although I was no longer being abused, I continued to dwell there. I was broken and deeply wounded and needed to be healed in my thoughts and my soul. As most people would run to a psychiatrist, I was drawn to the inner Voice and went to the Word, God's comforting and healing Word.

After everything about our homelife was revealed, we were sent to a psychologist. But after several months, I was worse than I was when I first started speaking to her. After a while, we begged to not go to her again. It was no help at all; instead, it was leaving us in a more confused state of pain. Rehearsing a pain and learning how to cope with it was not the answer. I wanted it gone—to be free from it all. The hunger and desperation for change were huge in me. My predicament was how to get to the safe place of freedom.

When you fight voices, the truth of the statement in Romans 12:2 can be overwhelming and seem impossible:

"Don't copy the behavior and customs of this world, but let God transform you into a new person by changing the way you think. Then you will learn to know God's will for you, which is good and pleasing and perfect."

Yet this was part of my hope and prayer to learn about God's will for me. Going to church, I would listen intently and then go home and look up the Scriptures for myself and pray for understanding. These tiny baby steps helped, yet I never really got it. Some people may stop after a few times thinking, "Oh, forget it, that doesn't work." But for me it burned inside me as if this reaching out to God was life or death; so I kept walking forward, hoping, believing I would understand it, see it, and feel it one day. And I did!

A VICTOR NOT A VICTIM

How do you renew your mind? How do you erase the thoughts you have known since birth? How do you not be as the world expects you to be? The world says, "It's okay, we understand. Accept the fact that you are a victim and that is your label for life. Let us give you a prescription to help you cope and numb the pain." I did not want to be conformed to that. I did not want to be known as a victim all of my life. I am not there anymore. The abuse is no longer taking place. Am I still a victim? Or, am I a victorious survivor? I chose to be victorious!

The world was trying to conform me to their way of thinking—and not until I refused that, sensing there was more, did I break from it. I did not want to follow the script the world wrote about how I should behave and think because of my childhood trauma. Understand it or not, I knew God was the only hope there was for me to be free. His Word slowly and completely washed me clean, and the renewing of my mind began. I learned to apply Matthew 6:34: *"So don't worry about tomorrow, for tomorrow will bring its own worries. Today's trouble is enough for today."*

The Scriptures teach that no one can come to the Lord unless the Spirit draws the person: *"For no one can come to me unless the Father who sent me draws them to me, and at the last day I will raise them up"* (John 6:44). The Holy Spirit is continually drawing people. Even at that point, you can ignore it or say no. For me, I was attracted and drawn to the Voice because it held for me what I hungered for, and that was deliverance, freedom, and a new name.

To renew your mind, you can truthfully only do it with the Word of God. This means continually being in the Word—whether you listen to it, read it, watch it, confess it, or all of the above. Renew your mind to know what God thinks of you, what He says about you. Just keep reading and ask the Holy Spirit to give you understanding, and I promise the Word will produce life in you, it will guard your heart, and wash you clean from the inside out. Your mind will become sound, and peace will come. No one ever fails when they reach for the Lord.

You may be thinking that I am making too much out of Jesus, and it simply doesn't work that way. You may think you have to be strong on your own; no one is going to help you through this life, let alone Jesus. Let me ask you, how do you know He can't help you through life? How long have you worked on it by yourself? Are you any better off on your own?

My life depends on Jesus telling the truth! I trust only Him, and He has never let me down. I tried to depend on humanity, but they continually let me down. You bet your sweet self, today and always Jesus is my tower of refuge, and I will continue to run to Him. When I began this journey for freedom, I leaned on Him, looked for help not only for my next breath but the next step. I was in desperate need of help. There was no pride or arrogance in me. My spirit was broken so much so that I prayed to die. Unknowingly at that time, the Lord had different, wonderful plans for me—and that is how I am positive He has different, wonderful plans for you.

MY FIRST BIBLE

As I mentioned, we were poor growing up. Clothes were hand-me-downs, shoes were one pair each, and if those wore out, we had none, and food was what we could afford unless it came to Dad, he had the best set aside for himself. Since there was no car, we walked everywhere, even to church. My mom worked two to three jobs to raise all of us, and our dad did nothing, except smoke, listen to his music, and abuse. He claimed he couldn't work because he was injured in the service. There were no visible injuries that anyone could see and to this day, there is no evidence that I can think to show he was in the service at all. Anyways, we could not afford a Bible for one of us, let alone all six children. Every Sunday, we would all walk ten miles to church along with my grandmother and aunt on my mom's side. We were raised with manners and girls were always ladies, and even though we had little, we took care of what we had and always looked our best going to church. During Sunday school, I never had a Bible, and someone would share with me. There was a woman at church who knew this and one day surprised us all with a gift of Bibles. I was still young, and mine was a children's Bible. The excitement is hard to express, except to say it was my precious possession. All of my hope was in it. I held it close and read it privately in my bedroom every night. I read it every night, but truthfully I understood none of it. I focused on the Old Testament and the stories. It was so complicated to understand that I never got past it to even get to the New Testament. Even without understanding or having anyone to teach me—the word is alive and powerful, and the Lord searches the heart—my heart was committed unto death to it. I just grabbed onto it and held on for dear life. If it said it, I believed it. My dad caught me often in my room with the door closed and reading my Bible. He got so angry one night, he grabbed it out of my hands and put it away and said, "I am sick and tired of seeing you read this trash," and he put it where I could not reach it. Eventually, I found it and was able to find a way to reach it and take it back. I still have that Bible to this day and in almost mint condition. Now and then I pick it up and look at it, open the front cover and look at the name of the person who gave it to me. Then I thank God for them and for delivering me from that time. I may not have understood it, but somehow the Word got into me and guarded my heart. It was that Voice in me that said NO and to reject what I was hearing about me.

There is a story I am reminded of about a little boy who was asked to do the impossible; frustrated he wanted to prove it was impossible, and his grandfather taught him a great lesson.

There was an old farmer and his grandson. This boy adored his grandfather and wanted to be just like him, so he mimicked everything he did. Every morning his grandfather sat at the kitchen table reading the Bible. The grandson did the same thing except he didn't understand most of what he read. The little he did understand, he forgot as he walked away. One day as his grandfather was putting coal in the stove, his grandson said, "Grandpa, I keep trying to read the Bible just like you, but I just don't understand it, and I forget the little I do get, so what good is it to read the Bible?"

The grandfather stopped what he was doing and picked up the empty coal basket and said, "Take this coal basket down to the river and bring back a basket of water." The grandson did as he was told, except by the time he got to the house, the basket was empty.

His grandfather chuckled and said, "You will have to move a little faster next time," and sent him back to the river with the basket to try again. This happened a few times with the same result. Tired and frustrated the boy suggested he take a bucket to go fetch the water. His grandfather said, "I don't want a bucket of water; I want a basket of water." You're just not trying hard enough. The boy made one last attempt, scooped the water up, and ran as fast as he could; nevertheless, the water leaked out before he returned to the house.

As he was catching his breath, he said, "See Grandpa, it's useless!"

The grandfather sat down with his grandson and said, "So you think it is useless?" Pointing to the basket, the grandfather said, "Look at the basket." The boy looked at the basket, and for the first time, he noticed that the basket didn't look the same. Instead, it was clean. You couldn't tell there was ever any coal carried in the basket. The grandfather said, "Son, that's what happens when you read the Bible. You might not understand or remember everything, but when you read it, it will transform you from the inside out." (Based on "The Bible and The Coal Basket," distributed by email; author unknown).

~

That basket could not hold the water, and it frustrated the boy, and he felt it was useless. But the grandfather said, "Oh, but look how clean the basket is." The Word of God will do the same for you. That is how God works in our lives when we stay in the Word. It changes us from the inside out, and it will slowly transform us into the image of His Son. Just keep reading it.

I did not understand what I was reading and the denomination I was raised in didn't help so I couldn't hold the water of the Word, yet it washed me clean. Friend, it works whether you understand it or not as long as your heart is right. It will wash you, cleanse you and keep you safe. It restores, refreshes, rejuvenates, and delivers without you understanding how. Let's reflect on Psalms 119:9-16 (MSG):

> *How can a young person live a clean life? By carefully reading the map of your Word. I'm single-minded in pursuit of you; don't let me miss the road signs you've posted. I've banked your promises in the vault of my heart*

so I won't sin myself bankrupt. Be blessed, GOD; train me in your ways of wise living. I'll transfer to my lips all the counsel that comes from your mouth; I delight far more in what you tell me about living than in gathering a pile of riches. I ponder every morsel of wisdom from you, I attentively watch how you've done it. I relish everything you've told me of life, I won't forget a word of it.

When you begin reading the Bible it may seem difficult. Just keep planting the seed into you and it will grow: *"Night and day, while he's asleep or awake, the seed sprouts and grows, but he does not understand how it happens"* (Mark 4:27).

When you garden, you plant seeds into the ground of precisely what you want to grow in your garden. You cannot plant sunflower seeds and expect roses to grow. It just will not happen. If you want sunflowers, you need several things: good fertile soil, sunflower seeds, sun, and water. You make sure you plant the seed in a good sunny location because it will need the sun to grow. This type of seed cannot be planted in the shade because it requires the sun as part of the nutrition. Once you plant the seed, you need to tend to it to make sure that it has plenty of water. It's the same for us. We are the fertile soil, the Word is the seed, and once the seed is planted, it needs to be tended to for it to grow. We need to continue to water that seed, and before long, it grows and produces fruit. We don't know how, but it works.

Now, you cannot plant the seed and then the next day dig it up and still expect the flower to grow. Likewise, we cannot go to church for an hour on Sunday, and then the rest of the week live in fear, doubt, and unbelief. You cannot go for the rest of the week without opening the Bible and reading it.

You need to be in it daily to keep the seed that was planted, fed, and watered. Jesus said, *"But if you remain in me and my words remain in you, you may ask for anything you want, and it will be granted!"* (John 15:7).

Don't worry about being smart enough to understand what you are reading. If your heart is thirsty enough for the truth, just keep at it and understanding will come. Anytime I sat down to read the Bible, I would ask the Holy Spirit to help me understand. He can also send people down your path to help teach you. Jesus is not expecting you to be a college graduate; he can give understanding to even an illiterate person. He only asks us to believe in Him. For most people, that seems too easy or simple, and therefore, it cannot be true.

If you have lived through what an abused child would have, you would not think that way; you would think, believe in Him? Why? How can I believe in someone I cannot even see when the people I can see have lied to me? Everyone I ever trusted and believed their words failed me. My parent broke the most precious treasure of trusting within me. How can I ever trust what anyone says? Understandably, it is not simple or easy for those of us who suffered or are suffering from the misguided trust. It has taken years, and I believe the rest of my life to build that in me ultimately. Even today, I will tell you I do not trust people, and you should never trust people. Is that shocking? I am a Christian. I learned to love people and trust God. What if I told you that not even Jesus trusted man? The Gospel of John shows us that Jesus didn't trust people because he knew all people: *"But Jesus didn't trust them, because he knew all about people. No one needed to tell him about human nature, for he knew what was in each person's heart"* (John 2:24-25).

He didn't need anyone to tell Him about human nature, for He knew what human nature was. If Jesus doesn't trust people, then why would we? I do not even trust myself. I love myself but trust: no. That may seem odd to believe of yourself, except you will never know how you will respond in any given situation until you are in it, and that is when what you believe comes to light. I never say that there is an area in my life I have a handle on. Until I am in that situation, I cannot know what the response will be.

Chapter 9

Taking Control of Your Thoughts

This chapter is a continuation of our discussion about how God renews your mind through His Word. Your brain, which holds your mind, is a powerful organ. It is connected to every part of your body. It has been proven that your thoughts can produce life or death in your physical body. Toxic thoughts can produce all kinds of sickness and disease. You do not have to be a rocket scientist to know that when you think of good things, you feel good, energetic, and joyful. And when you think negative thoughts, you feel tired and worn out. The biggest battleground you will face in life is the battle going on in your mind.

When you accepted Jesus as your Lord and Savior, your spirit was reborn, but not your mind. Don't be surprised that you still have the same thoughts and imaginations as you did before Jesus became part of your life. That is why He tells us to renew our minds (Romans 12:2).

When we are born, we are born with a spirit, soul, and body. We live in a physical body as long as we are in this world; within the body is our spirit. The spirit is the real you. We also have a soul. Our soul is made up of our mind, will, and emotions.

Before becoming believers, we were led by our soul. Now we have to learn to switch that around and be controlled by the spirit, not by our soul. We need to take control of our thoughts and not let everything fly through our minds unchecked. We need to wash our minds out with the Scriptures, God's Word.

You may not understand how to take control of your thoughts and change them. For someone to even dare ask you to do that can cause anxiety, and you may become overwhelmed. I understand that feeling. Let me encourage you and suggest starting by taking baby steps.

One thing I needed to learn was controlling what I allowed myself to think about. That is, not to let the thoughts rush through my mind unchecked. Learn how you think and what thoughts you allow to go through your mind. Millions of thoughts race through our minds consistently; so in order to get a handle on what I was thinking about all the time, I began to journal and write down my thoughts. Later I would go back and read my thoughts; that way I discovered what issues I needed to eliminate from my thought life—the biggest was fear.

Let me use fear as an example. In order to exchange my thoughts of fear for faith, courage, and hope, I found out what God says regarding it. I opened my Bible and read Scriptures on fear and wrote them down next to every toxic thought of fear. Then, when the thought of fear would come in any area, I would say "No, I refuse to fear." And then I would speak the

Scripture I had written down. This process of writing your thoughts can help evaluate yourself and then help you take positive steps to change the way you think.

Write down your thoughts and then later go back and read them. You will see a pattern develop. The next step is to exchange those thoughts or change those thoughts to a positive end. Because I was always fearful, I changed those thoughts to a positive means, telling myself, "I will no longer be afraid." Let's say you write your thoughts, and then after reading them, you find you worry all the time. Take that knowledge and find Scriptures about worry and what God says about it. I encourage you to write those Scripture verses in your journal.

For example, Matthew 6:34 tells us, *"Don't worry about tomorrow, for tomorrow will bring its own worries. Today's trouble is enough for today."* But you may say, "Well, what I'm worried about today is tomorrow." Then let's look at 1 Peter 5:7 as it says, *"Give all your worries and cares to God, for he cares about you."* So in your journal, write down the worry and then say, "I'm not going to worry about this, I give it to You, Jesus, because I was not created to worry and You will take care of it because You care for me."

Allow your mind and imagination to go there and see you giving that worry to Jesus. See Him take that care and make it all work out. When you give your worry to Jesus, you can't take it back, leave it in His capable and loving hands. This process is very powerful for me. It brings healing in many ways. You too will begin to renew your mind when you use this process to detox your thoughts, and the renewing of your mind will move along quickly.

Remember the saying, "If I say I can't, then I can't; if I say I can, then I can." *You* rule your thoughts. *You* choose to take that thought or dismiss it.

Let's use our minds and imaginations in a positive state. Writing things out helps. Even when I was angry with someone, this practice helped me. I would write out what I was thinking in a letter or email—but not send it. The next day I would reread it. Most of the time I would feel so silly because half of what I wrote didn't make any sense. So, I would throw out the letter or delete the email and be thankful that I didn't send it in anger and regret it the next morning. In the early days, this helped me learn to forgive people.

Before you know it, as you memorize Scriptures, God's Word will become part of you. As you go through your day, you can meditate on it and it will bring you peace: *"Study this Book of Instruction continually. Meditate on it day and night so you will be sure to obey everything written in it. Only then will you prosper and succeed in all you do"* (Joshua 1:8). If you choose Matthew 6:34 for worry, as you go through your day and a thought comes to make you worry, you can remind yourself of that Scripture and cast that thought of worry aside. That is how you can meditate on the Word of God day and night.

SPEAK POSITIVE THOUGHTS

Therefore take no thought, saying, What shall we eat? or, What shall we drink? or, Wherewithal shall we be clothed?

—Matthew 6:31 (KJV)

Let me focus on the first part of Matthew 6:31, *"Therefore take no thought, saying...."* Here is another mistake I used to fall into, saying negative thoughts out loud. We take the thought into our minds by saying it. It is known that the one voice we trust the most is our own. By saying those negative thoughts out loud, it would go into my mind and begin to convince me that it was true. Not until I learned this Scripture, that we should not say negative thoughts, could I stop them from haunting me. Speaking negativity sets our feet on a path of making those thoughts come to life. Our words produce life, so saying them directs our footsteps. Proverbs 4:23 says, *"Guard your heart above all else, for it determines the course of your life."*

Years ago I wondered, "If my words produce life or death, how do I change that?" My mind was filled with negative thoughts from the words my biological father spoke over me, even though my heart wanted to believe something good. It took a long time to break, but I learned to think and say what God thinks and says about me.

When you accept Jesus as your Lord and Savior, you are adopted into God's family and become His child. This was part of the repainting that the Lord took me through in the Father. This was what my earthly father was supposed to do. Now, I have a new Father, a heavenly, loving Father, and what He thinks about me is the truth. It was not easy, and at first I felt silly to do so, but every time I wanted to say the negative, I would instead say something God said about me—something from His Word. It didn't feel true at first because I was going against years of hearing hurtful and harmful words that were spoken over me.

Also, I searched the Bible and found the Scriptures that revealed who I am in Christ and would confess those Scriptures daily. My mind needed to be renewed (Romans 12:2), and the only way to change those thoughts was to say what God said about me. Because I naturally trusted my voice the most, as I confessed the Scriptures out loud, each one would sink into my heart and change began.

My emotions told me the opposite, as did my facial expressions, but I was desperate to change and break free. So, I could not go by my emotions; instead, I made the decision to change. I knew that feelings led me this way one day and another way the next day. If I wanted to change, there had to be no excuses; and I was sticking to eliminating negative talk from my vocabulary and renewing my mind. Maybe "resolved" is a better word. I was resolved and continued to stay in the Word. Let's read John 8:31-32: *"Jesus said to the people who believed in him, 'You are truly my disciples if you remain faithful to my teachings. And you will know the truth, and the truth will set you free.'"*

Eventually, my mind began to change, and my spirit began to come more alive; and slowly, my mind and spirit started to be in communion. My spirit was beginning to lead!

The war between my soul and spirit was constant. Therefore my self-talk was tough. I would constantly tell myself, "I'm not there any longer, stop it! Leave yesterday where it belongs—yesterday. Today is a new day." To change, you need to face the issue, work through it, and get over it. Stop living your life in shame based on what has happened to you or what you have done in the past. It's over! So let it go and get over it.

Take yourself to another level and see your past behind you, don't turn around to look at it, keep your face forward and keep walking. Take the high ground. Forgive yourself and others, and let it go. Let's ponder on 1 John 3:20-21: *"Even if we feel guilty, God is greater than our feelings, and he knows everything. Dear friends, if we don't feel guilty, we can come to God with bold confidence."*

NO MORE GUILT

Guilt is another feeling we suffer from as we come to the Lord. Even if your feelings are overwhelming, I encourage you to still approach the Lord. He already knows everything and will not reject you or cast you away. Jesus has paid the price for it all.

Scriptures teach that when you accept Jesus as Lord and Savior, you are born again and become a new creature, old things are passed away, and all things have become new. It's true! Read 2 Corinthians 5:17: *"This means that anyone who belongs to Christ has become a new person. The old life is gone; a new life has begun!"*

The problem is when we accept Jesus as Savior, we don't let go of the old life. Maybe salvation is made too simple without explanation of what happens when we receive the gift Jesus gives us. Nevertheless, we keep walking in the shame of the past, and that should not be. When we are born from our mother's womb, we are born with a body, spirit, and soul, and the sin nature is already inside us, thanks to Adam and Eve.

But after you receive Jesus as Lord and Savior, you are reborn. Not your physical body, but your spirit; and that means that sin nature is broken and no longer has power over you. Your spirit is now new with God's Spirit in you. Now, you still can sin if you so choose, but it has no control over you as it did before. After the experience of salvation, your spirit is new as a baby and of God. Hence the term "born again." You are now grafted into the family of God and accepted as one of His dear children.

A PROCESS OF CHANGE

Salvation is instant, but renewing your mind is a process. The problem left is the mind. That part does not get saved or reborn. That is why some people continue with their lives without making changes that bring them into the will of God. We are used to living by our minds with its ungodly thoughts; we are directed how to live, move, breathe, and think about people, and ourselves. What needs to be the next step is to renew our mind and start learning how to be led by our spirit, not our thoughts.

We live in a computer age, so perhaps this will help with a mental picture. If your computer's hard drive is full of garbage, it runs slowly, crashes, and eventually it breaks down. To fix it, you can take it to a computer geek to reset the hard drive and start it anew. When you get your computer back, it is as if it were brand-new, now you just have to be careful what you install on it to keep it running smoothly.

That is what it is like with our mind. It's full of all the garbage from our life thus far, and it runs slowly, crashes, and eventually breaks down. The Word will clean up the mind and bring new life, a new way of thinking, and break old habits and thoughts—God's Word resets it.

Essentially that is what you are doing, replacing negative, garbage thoughts and behaviors with new positive ones. You exchange the words you heard and learned all your life for the words and thoughts of God and how He genuinely thinks about you. It is as simple as taking what someone says, like, "You are worthless," and drowning out that falsehood with God's truth by saying, "No, I'm not!" According to the Bible, God says I am more precious than many sparrows. Jesus said in Luke 12:6-7,

> *What is the price of five sparrows—two copper coins? Yet God does not forget a single one of them. And the very hairs on your head are all numbered. So don't be afraid; you are more valuable to God than a whole flock of sparrows.*

An orphan child suffers from not being part of a family, as well; they can give us a picture of how salvation works. Orphans have no identity, yet they have labels attached to them. Many may have no parents, family, heritage, or perceived future. The world names them as unloved, unwanted, unworthy, lost, helpless, worthless, unadoptable, and the list goes on and sinks into their minds and hearts.

Then one day, a couple comes along and adopts them. How exciting, that people came together, looked at them, and said, "I want them!" What a wonderful feeling! Once the adoption is complete, they have an identity, heritage, new beginning in life, and a perceived future. Their past is there, but it doesn't matter anymore, because they identify with their new family. The past and heritage of the family that adopted them have now become their own—the same when you get adopted into the family of God. Your past is just that, the past. You now have a new name, past, and heritage of the family of God. Now you have to learn all about how the family works and how your new Father looks, sees, and thinks about you. He has adopted you into His family and has become your Father.

This knowledge, spiritual revelation, not only broke me but set me free. Because I had a cruel earthly father, I wanted to know what my heavenly Father was like. I found Him to be the Father who listens to me, loves me even if I make a mistake, and helps me through it. He is the One I can run to when times get tough and I need answers. And He's there for those moments when there is nothing to be said, but stays right by me as I cry myself to sleep. He gives me surprises in life by giving me the desires of my heart. I finally have a wonderful Father. This is precisely what I have found in God.

GOD IS LOVE

To be accepted and loved is a natural human need. It is not wrong to want that. Some people would say that it is just my imagination, and I live in a fantasy world. Fantasy has nothing to do with it. This is what I have experienced a father is by walking with the Lord, studying the Word, searching for the true meaning and understanding of what the Scripture says, and having a prayer life. I have felt the love, seen His love expressed toward me. You do not have to believe me, yet I am living proof of His love. For all of my days,

I will continually learn how good of a Father He is; and I am thankful.

Love is what God is, and if you were taught differently, they lied to you. His love is what is healing me. This new love slowly and tenderly has made me feel loved, acceptable, confident, and safe. We spend so much time labeling people with issues, we forget a significant healer—stop, listen, understand, and love. Love without judgment. It is powerful to love.

Too often we don't communicate, and people die more today from loneliness than any other age. We need to socialize face-to-face, listen genuinely, and try to understand people today more than ever. Even some of the younger group aren't being taught to respect and appreciate others like they should.

Too many times in today's society, we create shame with labels: "Here take this test and check your boxes," and after the doctor examines your answers, you're given a label. Then some try to comfort you by writing you a prescription so you can cope with your new knowledge of how messed up you are. Okay, you have this and here is a prescription, now go your way.

I believe this approach to life is a breakdown in human compassion. We have done away with sitting and listening to someone's story and helping the person work through it and deal with it. Instead, we label them as sick and keep them medicated. Now they walk in shame and guilt, which they are unable to cope with, because of the oppressive label. It becomes their identity, instead of God's accurate identification. The truth in the Word of God can give you worth and the identity you desire.

READ AND MEDITATE ON GOD'S WORD

Many people feel they do not have what it takes to understand the Bible. They complain they get lost after the first sentence. If that is you, first, I recommend that you read a good translation—one that you can understand. There are a variety of Bible versions I used in this book. You may want to try the New Living Translation, The Message, the Amplified Bible, or the New International Version. You may want to visit *www.biblegateway.com* to find the Bible version that best suits your reading and comprehension style.

The Bible says, if you lack understanding, ask God. Read James 1:5-8 (MSG):

> *If you don't know what you're doing, pray to the Father. He loves to help. You'll get his help, and won't be condescended to when you ask for it. Ask boldly, believingly, without a second thought. People who "worry their prayers" are like wind-whipped waves. Don't think you're going to get anything from the Master that way, adrift at sea, keeping all your options open.*

Let's also reflect on 2 Peter 1:2-4:

> *May God give you more and more grace and peace as you grow in your knowledge of God and Jesus our Lord. By his divine power, God has given us everything we need for living a godly life. We have received all of this by coming to know him, the one who called us to himself by means of his marvelous glory and excellence. And because of his glory and excellence, he has given us great and precious*

> *promises. These are the promises that enable you to share his divine nature and escape the world's corruption caused by human desires.*

Stay in the Word and everything you need to know you will learn from it. Begin to exchange old negative thoughts for new positive ones. This is your choice. Control your thoughts; don't just let them fly haphazardly into your mind. Stop and toss out the thoughts that do not conform to the Word of God. Meditate on the Scriptures and be okay to be alone with your thoughts and control them. The truth is, God will not leave you alone, He will be there with you, with every step you take.

One thing to know and remember is that what we learn in the Scriptures we need to apply in life. Do what you learn, don't just read God's Word: *"But don't just listen to God's word. You must do what it says. Otherwise, you are only fooling yourselves"* (James 1:22).

It is easy to fall back into our old ways because it is natural. If you want to change, you must do what the Bible says. Otherwise, change will not happen. Apply the things you learn and apply it to your life. Hear and do, that is what produces change. It's for you. Not someone else. You! Teach and train your mind how to think. Your spirit should control your mind and thoughts—don't allow your mind or emotions to rule you. Make a choice as Moses commanded the children of Israel in Deuteronomy 30:20:

> ***You can make this choice*** *by loving the LORD, your God, obeying him, and committing yourself firmly to him. This is the key to your life. And if you love and obey*

the LORD, you will live long in the land the LORD swore to give your ancestors Abraham, Isaac, and Jacob.

How do you do that? You may think that it is easier said than done. Well, I can tell you this is what worked for me. It is work, without a doubt. I would take Scriptures and confess them; stop and meditate on them; use them in my prayers; write them on post-it notes, and put them where they would remind me when I saw them. I would do that until it became part of me. If you do that repeatedly, it becomes part of your life. Your mind changes, your heart changes, and it produces change.

PRAISE AND WORSHIP

Another habit I formed was listening to and/or singing praise and worship songs. Singing praise and worship songs is a powerful tool for change. Not only is it a confession, but you are also meditating on the Lord and the words, the wholesome, godly words fill your heart. There are all types of praise and worship music, some with lyrics, some without. For me, singing with words worked wonders, and still does.

Christian music can take me from depression, shame, and discouragement. It breaks through any situation I'm facing. By the time I'm done, my focus is on Jesus, the problem doesn't seem so big, and my whole being is changed to being calmer, happier, stronger, and encouraged. When singing isn't appropriate, listen to Christian music on the radio, your phone, or the television. The music will sink into your mind and heart and you can even sing yourself to sleep at night knowing that God is with you. God inhabits the praises of His children.

Even King Saul was soothed with music by David. First Samuel 16:14-23 record this in the Old Testament:

> *Now the Spirit of the* LORD *had left Saul, and the* LORD *sent a tormenting spirit that filled him with depression and fear. Some of Saul's servants said to him, "A tormenting spirit from God is troubling you. Let us find a good musician to play the harp whenever the tormenting spirit troubles you. He will play soothing music, and you will soon be well again." "All right," Saul said. "Find me someone who plays well, and bring him here." One of the servants said to Saul, "One of Jesse's sons from Bethlehem is a talented harp player. Not only that—he is a brave warrior, a man of war, and has good judgment. He is also a fine-looking young man, and the* LORD *is with him." So Saul sent messengers to Jesse to say, "Send me your son David, the shepherd." Jesse responded by sending David to Saul, along with a young goat, a donkey loaded with bread, and a wineskin full of wine. So David went to Saul and began serving him. Saul loved David very much, and David became his armor bearer. Then Saul sent word to Jesse asking, "Please let David remain in my service, for I am very pleased with him." And whenever the tormenting spirit from God troubled Saul, David would play the harp. Then Saul would feel better, and the tormenting spirit would go away.*

There has been music since the beginning of time, and it is daily heard in Heaven. The book of Psalms is a book of songs as is the book Song of Solomon. There are many examples of singing praise and worship in the Bible. Jesus and His disciples sang hymns (Matthew 26:30). The apostle Paul encouraged the Ephesian believers to sing psalms and hymns: *"Be filled with the Holy Spirit, singing psalms and hymns and spiritual songs among yourselves, and making music to the Lord in your hearts"* (Ephesians 5:18b-19).

I can probably guess that today if your favorite song comes on the radio, you stop everything, turn up the sound, and sing at the top of your lungs without regret. So why should praise and worship songs be any different? It is what we give our hearts to that matters. When you start listening to praise and worship music, you will feel exhilarated and joyful.

Don't allow society to tell you what to do, that believers are wasting their time. Your mind will provide all sorts of reasons as to what would be more productive: the dishes, laundry, watching TV, and so on. The conclusion is that praising God is never a waste of our time. Caring for your well-being is never a waste of time. The world's way of coping with life's challenges was not enough for me. Singing soothes, takes me away from the daily grind, and changes my focus. As time went on, I found as I slept, the songs would be singing to me. Today, I find myself singing or humming a melody for no reason, and my spirit is happy.

OUR RESPONSIBILITY

Ultimately, it is my responsibility to control my thoughts, conversations, and imagination; no one else could or can do it for me, only me. Realizing that, my thoughts calmed down.

They weren't racing. I could take hold of them. And I could destroy the old tapes of the voices of those who tore me down. My strength was building on the inside out. I began to walk more confidently and know my true identity.

It is the same in every area of life. We have the responsibility for what we eat, drink, speak, hate, and so on. Let's take swearing for an example. Today, swearing has become part of everyday language, male and female; and it is considered an acceptable practice. I am not condemning people, it is just a manner of expression to them, so I understand and it doesn't faze me. My belief is, though, we can say the same thing without using those words that have no meaning; instead, they tear down and belittle. Scriptures tell us not to let any unwholesome speech come out of our mouths: ***"Don't use foul or abusive language.*** *Let everything you say be good and helpful, so that your words will be an encouragement to those who hear them"* (Ephesians 4:29).

I lose respect for priests, pastors, and Christians who swear with every other word and then on Sunday say, "Praise Jesus. Hallelujah!" Are you kidding? And really, I didn't have to force myself not to swear; God's Word washed me from swearing. Those words were no longer part of my vocabulary.

When I was a child, I swore. Of course, that language was spoken everywhere, including my home. My grandmother once heard me and said, "Don't swear, that is unbecoming for a lady." And she was right. I agree with that statement; I am a queen and priest in the making, and it is unacceptable for a child of the highest King to speak that way. You can see that role of ours in Revelation 5:10 (KJV): *"And hast made us unto our God kings and priests: and we shall reign on the earth."*

All of that to say, if you want to transform yourself from being afraid or alone or stuck in an unhealthy situation, you have to decide you want to change. Not just say you want it or wish to have it; instead, be resolved in your decision. Decide, even if you have a rough day, are tired, or feeling emotional, you will still move forward toward change. If all you can do in those moments is keep your mouth shut, then do that. You will make mistakes and flub it up now and again, just don't let that get you down; repent and let it go and keep walking ahead.

For me, the Word of God took a young child that was broken into pieces not wanting to live and it picked me up, cleaned, rebuilt, and molded me into a child of His very own. No more voices were trying to come back and taunt me. I now have peace in my mind—devastation to restoration, a woman restored.

CHOOSING TO CHANGE

You can't want to change for five days and then say, "Forget it, that doesn't work." I admit that it was hard at first and painful without a doubt. It was a fight and a battle of mind and will. I didn't know if I would make it, but I determined I was going to set myself free, with God's help! I was absolute in my decision. Did I cry? Yes! Did I want to quit? Yes! I even cried to God that I couldn't do it. But then I got up and stopped pitying myself and continued.

Today, there is no fight. I face challenges from time to time and can get discouraged, but instead of entertaining any negative thoughts, I go into praise and worship, pray, read the Scriptures, or listen to a program or an audiobook. I make myself move away from the negativity and not stay in that state of mind. When others may ask the doctor to give them a prescription for the pain to stop, my drug, recovery recipe, and salve for my wounds is to think positively—focus on Jesus and His love and mercy. He does it all. He is my cure for all. Sometimes it takes a bit for me to refocus; nevertheless, I am steadfast and resolved to remain on the path of righteousness.

Some say what I did is too much work. They would rather go to doctors to get prescriptions, psychologists to analyze them, become alcoholics or drug addicts, food addicted, and so on. But my way keeps me in tune with my heavenly Father, I recover naturally, not with drugs or chemicals. Nothing is wrong with seeking treatment from doctors, so please don't misunderstand me; if you think you need a doctor, see one.

It seems, though, to be the way our society is today—give me a quick fix, numb the pain NOW!—not understanding the long-term effects. Many people are willing to do all or some of that, yet think it is too much work to sit and read the Scriptures, pray, and or listen to music?

Because God is the One who created me and knows me better than I do myself, I cannot think of anyone better to seek for a solution to my troubles. There may be times when I have to be corrected when I go to Him, but better now than later, I say. And He doesn't condemn me when I go to Him about a mistake, or He brings something to my attention that needs to change. He usually reveals His way through His Word. He never condemns, but lovingly has a conversation and explains, then leaves the rest to me. I can choose to follow that advice or ignore it—I decide to go His route. I have already experienced the opposite way that leads to more pain and heartache.

If you are not resolved in your decision to follow God and His way out, you will fail. Give yourself no room to back out or back down—no giving up and throwing in the towel. I used to tell myself, quitting is not an option. And if you want it, quitting is not an option for you either. It is your mind, and you are in control of it. You can help yourself and you must!

The way to get rid of shame and sin consciousness and the feeling of unworthiness is to look at Jesus. Look at Him and say, "God, it is because of what Jesus did that makes me worthy, and I believe You love me."

Purge your conscious by looking at the love of Jesus and what He did for you.

Go from knowing *of* Him to *knowing* Him.

The following are some Scriptures as examples:

Psalms 94:19 says, *"When doubts filled my mind, your comfort gave me renewed hope and cheer."* When you fill your mind with the Word, it comforts and renews hope and brings joy back into your life. In other words, it brings you back to yourself and who you are in Christ. Let's now talk about Romans 8:5-6 because this Scripture teaches us something important:

> *Those who are dominated by the sinful nature think about sinful things, but those who are controlled by the*

Holy Spirit think about things that please the Spirit. So letting your sinful nature control your mind leads to death. But letting the Spirit control your mind leads to life and peace.

Let me explain again that you are a spirit. The real you is spirit. You also have a soul, which consists of your mind, will, and emotions. Your mind and imagination are very powerful. Your mind can take one thought along with the imagination and make it into a huge deal to the point where you are convinced and will act upon it.

Don't let anyone mislead you in this area. Where do you spend most of your time? In your thoughts—the head (your mind and imagination) directs the body. You tell your foot to kick, and it will obey, or tell your hand to lift the spoon to your mouth, and it does. So if you focus on pornography, what is involved? It goes through the eyes to your mind and imagination, and the body responds. And your mind cannot erase those images. Consequently, that one time leads to another, and eventually you want more and more. Before you know it, you are watching, focusing, and imagining all kinds of sexual perversion. You are now dominated by it. It will be a matter of time before you act on those impulses and look at the opposite sex in that manner.

REAL LOVE

It is the same for everything else as well. What you focus on will direct and produce in your life. If you spend your time reading the Word, listening to or confessing it, where will your mind and imagination be? God's Word will dominate you and renew your mind and spirit, and lead and direct your life. Before you know it, you will see people differently. You will have love, compassion, and forgiveness in your heart; and as time goes by, people will say, "What's different about you?" You can look back and see the transformation. Now you're being led by the Holy Spirit and you think about what pleases the Spirit, which produces life.

By focusing on our new life in Jesus, we will experience God's peace in our hearts and minds: *"Then you will experience God's peace, which exceeds anything we can understand. His peace will guard your hearts and minds as you live in Christ Jesus"* (Philippians 4:7). Think about that for a moment—peace in your heart and mind. When I was a child, I thought and reasoned like a child, but if we don't deal with the wounds of our minds from our childhood abuse, we will never put away those childish mindsets. We need to renew our minds and grow up spiritually and emotionally, washing our minds of previous thoughts and thinking clean thoughts. We cannot do that without the Word of God.

Jesus can understand and relate to mental anguish since He went through it Himself. People He loved rejected Him: *"He was despised and rejected by mankind, a man of suffering, and familiar with pain"* (Isaiah 53:3a NIV). He was rejected by those He poured His life into. And in the Garden of Gethsemane He prayed for *"this cup of suffering"* to be taken from Him (Luke 22:42).

Crucifixion was the cruelest type of execution. Jesus anguished as we see in Luke 22:44: *"He prayed more fervently, and he was in such agony of spirit that his sweat fell to the ground like great drops of blood."* How He experienced the mental anguish of taking all the sins of humanity on Himself? Can you even imagine His thoughts? The sufferings of Jesus were far greater than anything we will ever go through in this life, yet Jesus suffered for us. He did it all because of His love for us. He is not waiting until you can love Him. He loved us first so we could love Him in return: *"**This is real love**—not that we loved God, but that he loved us and sent his Son as a sacrifice to take away our sins"* (1 John 4:10).

Love is who we are. We are created in God's image and *"God is love"* (1 John 4:8b). So we carry that spirit in us. *"We love each other because he loved us first"* (1 John 4:19). He is also the Creator and we carry that spirit in us. We violate His will when we think outside of His love. We are created to love—ourselves, others, and above all, God.

Chapter 10

Repentance

Jesus answered them, "Healthy people don't need a doctor—sick people do. I have come to call not those who think they are righteous, but those who know they are sinners and need to repent."
—Luke 5:31-32

The definition of "repentance" in Wikipedia is the activity of reviewing one's actions and feeling contrition or regret for past wrongs, which is accompanied by a commitment to change for the better.

The real definition of the word "repentance" means: to change your mind. To exchange your way of thinking for God's way of thinking. That change of mind would also result in the shift in your actions.

Repentance is one of those Christian words that puzzles people. Do you need to repent to be saved? Religion has taught that repentance means to turn away and stop sinning then come to Jesus. If that is true, then people will not come to Jesus. It is an impossible thought to repent of everything you did wrong in your life and to stop sinning. What if you miss something? Will your salvation then be null and void? What if you are doing something you do not think is a sin, but God does? Is it the Ten Commandments that I should be sorry for breaking? There are so many different thoughts being taught that people get confused.

Religion teaches that you have to stop sinning, repent of those sins, and then come to Jesus and you can be saved. They follow that with saying, but you better get your act together; otherwise, you will lose your salvation. For people who are used to living the world's way, that is impossible and they say, "No thank you, I know I can't do that." At that point, people go on living without hope that God would ever accept them because of all of the horrible things they have done.

Repentance is not a work. You don't clean yourself before taking a shower, you go to the shower to get clean. Likewise, don't try to get yourself fixed up before going to Christ; go directly to Christ, and He makes you clean. Go straight to Jesus just as you are.

Belief in Him brings change. That change, from my perspective, takes a lifetime. You continually learn what sin is as you grow and learn more in your spiritual walk with the Lord. So when you come to Jesus, you don't work to be worthy—Jesus makes you worthy. You need to rest in what Jesus has done for you.

The Gospel of John is the most preached and the most published book of the Bible. It is a book of salvation and the love of God. However, John 20:31 uses the word "believe," not repenting, to receive salvation: *"But these are written so that you may* *continue to **believe** that Jesus is the Messiah, the Son of God, and that by **believing** in him you will have life by the power of his name."*

John never once uses the word "repent." He uses the word "believe." It's all about believing. The word "believe" is used 85 times in the Gospel of John. You cannot believe without repenting. Believing is repentance. As you start to believe something, your understanding is growing, faith comes alive, and you change your mind from one way of thinking to another way of thinking.

Repentance means you changed your mind. Don't make repentance a work. You make it a work when you feel you have to get your life straight before going to Jesus. Don't "hope" to get into Heaven. You don't have to work all of your life to be acceptable and hopefully make it into Heaven. God will welcome you with open arms if you *believe* that Jesus is the Son of God (Titus 2:11).

God does not change His mind. He is the same always and forever. So don't mix the message. You do not *work* toward salvation. You *believe* unto salvation. We are to glorify Jesus, not humans. Works are people's way. Salvation is Jesus. It is by grace you are saved. Apostle Paul wrote in Ephesians 2:8-9, *"God saved you by his grace when you believed. And you can't take credit for this; it is a gift from God. Salvation is not a reward for the good things we have done, so none of us can boast about it."*

SALVATION

Some teach a dual message saying, "You need to repent of your sins or turn from your sins and accept Jesus Christ, and you will be saved." This teaching is just as wrong.

So we have to do work before getting saved? No. If it is true that we have to repent or turn away from sin first, then no one is saved. Who can stop sinning? No one—we are sinners, human beings who sin. We don't even know everything that is a sin. We continually discover what sin is, even if we have been saved for thirty years, we are still learning what sin is.

You don't want to sin, but you do. The Scriptures say that whatever is not of faith is sin (Romans 14:23 KJV), and to him who knows to do good and does it not to him, it is a sin (James 4:17). To preach this is "works salvation." But salvation is about what Christ did at the cross, not what we can do to earn salvation. Salvation is a gift, and the gift transforms you from inside out.

You cannot become a better man or woman to get saved. If so, then what would be good enough? The truth is, you are saved to become a better man or woman. People are turning away from salvation because of this perverted teaching. There is no middle ground in coming to salvation. You come to Jesus just as you are.

The Bible teaches that repentance means to change your mind. Have you ever made a decision and then later changed your mind? That is the repentance—you change your mind, your way of thinking. Changing your mind can be done without work or effort. You may be changing your mind or repenting right now as you read this book.

JESUS'S GIFT

Nor is repentance feeling sorry for your sins. It is not a feeling of remorse. Those are momentary feelings, and you can do all that and still go to hell. It's not about what you can do to get right with God. It's all about Jesus and His gift to you. Remember, you don't get clean before taking a shower; you go to the shower to become cleaned. Now, when you go into the shower, you use soap to help wash away all the dirt and grim. The same way after salvation, you are using the Word of God to wash you clean. You are cleaning yourself from the inside out.

Coming to salvation can produce crying, sadness, or joy, but emotions have nothing to do with receiving your salvation. As mentioned previously, I have witnessed a person who showed no emotion when he accepted Jesus as Lord and Savior and when he went home, his life was completely changed. I have also seen people who screamed, yelled, threw themselves on the floor and made a scene, claiming to have been saved; yet their lives showed absolutely no change at all.

Now I am not saying the reverse doesn't happen, it does—each person is different, the emotion can come, and it can be sincere, but no emotion is necessary. It is believing and confessing, not a feeling. What I am saying is, do not go by appearance; God doesn't. He goes by the heart: *"But **I, the LORD, search all hearts** and examine secret motives. I give all people their due rewards, according to what their actions deserve"* (Jeremiah 17:10). Read also 1 Samuel 16:7: *"But the LORD said to Samuel, 'Don't judge by his appearance or height, for I have rejected him. The LORD doesn't see things the way you see them. People judge by outward appearance, but **the LORD looks at the heart**.'"*

Also, don't be led astray if some Christians pull you aside and give you a list of rules of dos and don'ts. That will bring you back to a works mentality. Look at what apostle Paul says in Colossians 2:20-23:

You have died with Christ, and he has set you free from the spiritual powers of this world. So why do you keep on following the rules of the world, such as, "Don't handle! Don't taste! Don't touch!"? Such rules are mere human teachings about things that deteriorate as we use them. These rules may seem wise because they require strong devotion, pious self-denial, and severe bodily discipline. But they provide no help in conquering a person's evil desires.

I can show you many Christians who look like they have it all together, but inside they are dark as dark can get: *"This people draweth nigh unto me with their mouth, and honoureth me with their lips;* **but their heart is far from me**" (Matthew 15:8 KJV).

As it may seem repentance and salvation is too easy, even so not everyone will accept the gift. If Jesus told us to do something hard, we would understand, but He told us to believe and receive the gift of salvation. He has done all the rest for you. Some people say that is too easy. I say, "Thank You, Jesus, for making it easy, because I am bound to mess it up on my own."

There are people who to their last breath will not believe and receive the salvation gift because it was too easy. As humans, we understand punishment and believe we need to get punished for what we do wrong; if there is no punishment, there is no hope. Why? I think it is out of pride: "I won't let anyone pay the price for me! I will do it all by myself!" That is pride. God said through His prophet, *"But I, the LORD, search all hearts and examine secret motives"* (Jeremiah 17:10a).

In order to fully explain this gift, the following are some examples from the Bible.

In Luke 15:11-32, Jesus tells the story of the prodigal son:

To illustrate the point further, Jesus told them this story: "A man had two sons. The younger son told his father, 'I want my share of your estate now before you die.' So his father agreed to divide his wealth between his sons. A few days later this younger son packed all his belongings and moved to a distant land, and there he wasted all his money in wild living. About the time his money ran out, a great famine swept over the land, and he began to starve. He persuaded a local farmer to hire him, and the man sent him into his fields to feed the pigs. The young man became so hungry that even the pods he was feeding the pigs looked good to him. But no one gave him anything. When he finally came to his senses, he said to himself, 'At home even the hired servants have food enough to spare, and here I am dying of hunger! I will go home to my father and say, "Father, I have sinned against both heaven and you, and I am no longer worthy of being called your son. Please take me on as a hired servant."' So he returned home to his father. And while he was still a long way off, his father saw him coming. Filled with love and compassion, he ran to his son, embraced him, and kissed him. His son said to him, 'Father, I have sinned against both heaven and you, and I am no longer worthy of being called your son.' But his father said to the servants, 'Quick! Bring the finest robe in the house and put it on him. Get a ring for his finger and sandals for his feet. And kill the calf we have been fattening. We must celebrate with a feast, for this son of mine was dead and has now returned to life. He was lost, but now he is found.' So the party began. Meanwhile, the older son was in the fields working. When he returned home, he heard music and dancing in the house, and he asked one of the servants what was going on. 'Your brother is back,' he was told, 'and your father has killed the fattened calf. We are celebrating because of his safe return.' The older brother was angry and wouldn't go in. His father came out and begged him, but he replied, 'All these years I've slaved for you and never once refused to do a single thing you told me to. And in all that time you never gave me even one young goat for a feast with my friends. Yet when this son of yours comes back after squandering your money on prostitutes, you celebrate by killing the fattened calf!' His father said to him, 'Look, dear son, you have always stayed by me, and everything I have is yours. We had to celebrate this happy day. For your brother was dead and has come back to life! He was lost, but now he is found!'"

The story of the prodigal son is taught by some to mean that the boy lost his salvation and came back. But many others and I believe differently. What does the Scripture say as to why he left his father's house? His motives were greed and selfishness. It does not say he rejected his father or his beliefs; he still believed in his father. He just didn't want to wait until his father died to get his inheritance—he wanted it now. What an insult to his father, but notice his father didn't respond in kind; instead, he gave his son his inheritance and let him go.

Then later, when the son spent it and lost all his friends, he crashed and burned. With no food to eat, pig slop even looked appealing to him. When he came to his senses, he went back to his father, hoping to work as a hired hand. As his father saw him approaching, he ran to him to welcome him home.

Even though his son tried to repent and beg for forgiveness, his dad said right away to his servants to bring his son new, clean clothes and for them to get ready for a fabulous feast!

Now I ask you, what was the prodigal son's reason for coming back to his father? Because he repented for his sins? Did he miss his father? No! He came back because he needed food and shelter; he was hungry and had no place to live.

Even in John, we see Jesus revealing the truth of why some followed Him: *"Jesus replied, 'I tell you the truth, you want to be with me because I fed you, not because you understood the miraculous signs'"* (John 6:26).

You see, it doesn't matter why you come to your heavenly Father, only that you do. When you come toward Jesus, He will run toward you with arms wide open. That is our God!

Another example of repentance is being remorseful and making restitution. But what about Judas? Concerning him Matthew 27:3 says, *"When Judas, who had betrayed him, realized that Jesus had been condemned to die, he was filled with remorse. So he took the thirty pieces of silver back to the leading priests and the elders."*

Judas was remorseful; and not only that, he also gave the money back. So wasn't that restitution? People teach this is salvation. But what did Judas do right after that? He committed suicide by hanging himself (Matthew 27:5). Remorse and restitution aren't enough—we must freely accept by grace our salvation.

As Christians, we cannot undo what Adam did. Likewise, we cannot undo what the last Adam (Jesus) did either. We can reject all of what Jesus has done, or we can receive what He has done. It has nothing to do with remorse or restitution.

My curiosity gets me thinking about what would have happened if Judas would have waited and gone to Jesus. Judas never went to Jesus. If he would have waited for Jesus to complete God's will on earth, Jesus would have hung for him. He would never have had to hang for himself.

Some people may say, "I would rather die than receive forgiveness." Then some say, "How can we do this for free? We have to do our part!" No, that is bringing God's free gift of salvation back to works, and it ceases being a gift.

Let me ask you, when someone gives you a gift, what do you have to do? You have to receive it. Most often, you receive it with joy, maybe even tears and humility. You accept it and say thank you. Yet there are people who will reject your gift out of spite or pride, and because they believe in their hearts they are hurting you. It's true; I have experienced it. Yet they, in reality, hurt themselves.

The same is true with the gift Jesus offers. People accept it for what it is—the perfect gift of life—and say thank you. But others reject the gift when you offer it, thinking they know better than you, or Jesus. They think they are cutting you, but they are cutting themselves off from abundant life in Christ. Don't take it personally. Salvation has nothing to do with you. It has everything to do with Jesus.

An example of accepting salvation is Cornelius. This Scripture never uses the word "repent," it says whoever *believes* will receive: *"He [Jesus] is the one all the prophets testified about,* *saying that everyone who **believes** in him will have their sins forgiven through his name"* (Acts 10:43).

How about Mary who washed Jesus's feet with her tears and dried them with her hair. Did she say a word? The Gospel of Luke records the incident: *"Then she knelt behind him at his feet, weeping. Her tears fell on his feet, and she wiped them off with her hair. Then she kept kissing his feet and putting perfume on them"* (Luke 7:38). Did Jesus say, "Woman, stop, you first need to repent of your sins before you can expect Me to forgive you and accept you into the family." No, He did not.

Another salvation with repenting is when Jesus met the Samaritan woman. The story is told in John 4:1-42:

> *Jesus knew the Pharisees had heard that he was baptizing and making more disciples than John (though Jesus himself didn't baptize them—his disciples did). So he left Judea and returned to Galilee. He had to go through Samaria on the way. Eventually he came to the Samaritan village of Sychar, near the field that Jacob gave to his son Joseph. Jacob's well was there; and Jesus, tired from the long walk, sat wearily beside the well about noontime. Soon a Samaritan woman came to draw water, and Jesus said to her, "Please give me a drink." He was alone at the time because his disciples had gone into the village to buy some food. The woman was surprised, for Jews refuse to have anything to do with Samaritans. She said to Jesus, "You are a Jew, and I am a Samaritan woman. Why are you asking me for a drink?" Jesus replied, "If you only knew the gift God has for you and who you are speaking to, you would ask me, and I would give you living water." "But sir, you don't have a rope or a bucket," she said, "and this well is very deep.*

Where would you get this living water? And besides, do you think you're greater than our ancestor Jacob, who gave us this well? How can you offer better water than he and his sons and his animals enjoyed?" Jesus replied, "Anyone who drinks this water will soon become thirsty again. But those who drink the water I give will never be thirsty again. It becomes a fresh, bubbling spring within them, giving them eternal life." "Please, sir," the woman said, "give me this water! Then I'll never be thirsty again, and I won't have to come here to get water." "Go and get your husband," Jesus told her. "I don't have a husband," the woman replied. Jesus said, "You're right! You don't have a husband—for you have had five husbands, and you aren't even married to the man you're living with now. You certainly spoke the truth!" "Sir," the woman said, "you must be a prophet. So tell me, why is it that you Jews insist that Jerusalem is the only place of worship, while we Samaritans claim it is here at Mount Gerizim, where our ancestors worshiped?" Jesus replied, "Believe me, dear woman, the time is coming when it will no longer matter whether you worship the Father on this mountain or in Jerusalem. You Samaritans know very little about the one you worship, while we Jews know all about him, for salvation comes through the Jews. But the time is coming—indeed it's here now—when true worshipers will worship the Father in spirit and in truth. The Father is looking for those who will worship him that way. For God is Spirit, so those who worship him must worship in spirit and in truth." The woman said, "I know the Messiah is coming—the one who is called Christ. When he comes, he will explain everything to us." Then Jesus told her, "I AM the Messiah!" Just then his disciples came back. They were shocked to find him talking to a woman, but none of them had the nerve to ask, "What do you want with her?" or "Why are you talking to her?" The woman left her water jar beside the well and ran back to the village, telling everyone, "Come and see a man who told me everything I ever did! Could he possibly be the Messiah?" So the people came streaming from the village to see him....Many Samaritans from the village believed in Jesus because the woman had said, "He told me everything I ever did!" When they came out to see him, they begged him to stay in their village. So he stayed for two days, long enough for many more to hear his message and believe. Then they said to the woman, "Now we believe, not just because of what you told us, but because we have heard him ourselves. Now we know that he is indeed the Savior of the world."

We can learn a great deal from this story, but let's stay with the subject of repentance and salvation. Did Jesus tell the woman to repent of her adultery or she was going to hell? No, because it is not there. Jesus never asked her to repent and yet He knew full well all of her sins. He named her sins, and yet there was no condemnation in His words. Instead, He offered her life.

She wanted it immediately and was so excited she left her water pots there and ran into the village to tell everyone about Jesus. Because of her testimony, they opened their hearts to hear Jesus for themselves and more came to salvation.

Let's look at Abraham.

Abraham never repented of his sins. Abraham is known for his faith and obedience to God. The Scriptures say that Abraham believed God and it was counted unto him as righteousness. There is so much more to Abraham if you read his story. Abraham made a lot of mistakes, and his family was not known for their integrity. Abraham married his half-sister, and even back then it was a sin unto death. Twice he gave his wife to two kings to save his skin; and both times, God intervened before the kings made a mistake. Nevertheless, when God dealt with or spoke of Abraham, He never brought up his mistakes when he finally got to where God wanted him to be. God always spoke of Abraham as He saw him, whole and complete. He spoke of him from the standpoint of the result, not where he was presently.

There is also the example of the woman caught in adultery told in John 8:1-11:

> *Jesus returned to the Mount of Olives, but early the next morning he was back again at the Temple. A crowd soon gathered, and he sat down and taught them. As he was speaking, the teachers of religious law and the Pharisees brought a woman who had been caught in the act of adultery. They put her in front of the crowd. "Teacher," they said to Jesus, "this woman was caught in the act of adultery. The law of Moses says to stone her. What do you say?" They were trying to trap him into saying something they could use against him, but Jesus stooped down and wrote in the dust with his finger. They kept demanding an answer, so he stood up again and said, "All right, but let the one who has never sinned throw the first stone!" Then he stooped down again and wrote in the dust. When the accusers heard this, they slipped away one by one, beginning with the oldest, until only Jesus was left in the middle of the crowd with the woman. Then*

> *Jesus stood up again and said to the woman, "Where are your accusers? Didn't even one of them condemn you?" "No, Lord," she said. And Jesus said, "Neither do I. Go and sin no more."*

Jesus never condemned her, even though He knew her sin. Never once did He ask her to repent; instead, He said neither do I condemn you, go and sin no more. He forgave her sin and told her to stop it. She never says a word and goes her way.

It doesn't matter what your education level is or what side of the tracks you come from, nor the amount in your bank accounts. Salvation is for every living breathing person—regardless of what you are guilty or ashamed of from your past or present lives. Jesus has paid the price for it all.

The true preaching of the gospel produces right believing and changes your mind, then that revelation guides your life, and you will live right. Accept the simple truth of the gospel. If you are a seasoned Christian, don't try to show how knowledgeable you are. Don't conjure up anything. Jesus gave us what to say. Then people will come to salvation and want it sincerely. Not out of coercion but out of need. Follow the example of Jesus.

INSINCERE REPENTANCE

There can be insincere repentance. For example, during some crusades where they are preaching the salvation message, members of their team are spread out in the crowd. When the altar call is given, sometimes the team members may pressure people to say the prayer of repentance. That prayer meant nothing to them except a way of escape. There is such a thing as insincere or hollow repentance. Apostle Paul wrote in 2 Corinthians 7:10-11,

> *For the **kind of sorrow God wants** us to experience leads us away from sin and results in salvation. There's no regret for that kind of sorrow. But **worldly sorrow, which lacks repentance**, results in spiritual death. Just see what this godly sorrow produced in you! Such earnestness, such concern to clear yourselves, such indignation, such alarm, such longing to see me, such zeal, and such a readiness to punish wrong. You showed that you have done everything necessary to make things right.*

How do you know if you have worldly sorrow or godly sorrow? Worldly sorrow is when people get caught doing something wrong and realize they have to suffer the consequences for it. If they never got caught, they would not think about it again. It is only because they were caught that they feel sorry.

For me, false repentance is when someone says the prayer out of pressure and then tries to be spiritual, but keeps looking back and longing for the old way of life. They miss the things of their past life, and the pull is so strong they go back. Luke 9:62 says, *"But Jesus told him, 'Anyone who puts a hand to the plow and then looks back is not fit for the Kingdom of God.'"*

Religious people will push others into the salvation prayer without giving them time for them to reflect and consider their decision. That makes the prayer hollow, and then once they try to live the life, they have regret. That is one reason why I do not force people to say a prayer; I rather they come to me when they are ready for the prayer. It's better if I plant seeds and let them consider and research it for themselves. Then when they believe, and faith rises, they do not need me to say the prayer with them, anyone can, or they can pray all by themselves. That is a life-transforming prayer that will last. It is all about heart.

This is not to say that you will not feel temptation after you are saved. The flesh and spirit will always be at war with each other:

> *The sinful nature wants to do evil, which is just the opposite of what the Spirit wants. And the Spirit gives us desires that are the opposite of what the sinful nature desires. These two forces are constantly fighting each other, so you are not free to carry out your good intentions* (Galatians 5:17).

And there will be times where you fail as a Christian. But don't lose hope when it happens. Reflect on 1 John 1:9 (NLV): *"If we tell Him our sins, He is faithful and we can depend on Him to forgive us of our sins. He will make our lives clean from all sin."*

Be careful not to crucify a fellow Christian who fell to sin. Nothing angers me more than when I see Christians who persecute another Christian who genuinely is saved but got caught in a trap of temptation and fell to sin. Who are we to judge them? Unless we are placed in that situation and walked in their shoes, we have no idea how we would respond. Instead, we need to help other believers. This is what Galatians 6:1 (NLV) teaches: *"Christian brothers, if a person is found doing some sin, you who are stronger Christians should lead that one back into the right way. Do not be proud as you do it. Watch yourself, because you may be tempted also."*

Someone who truly repented will hate sin. Others who may have said the prayer don't hate sin, and don't want to get caught. One will want to give glory to God and feel remorse when they fail; the other is not concerned about God, but rather about getting caught. Consider John 3:20-21 (NLV):

> *Everyone who sins hates the Light. He stays away from the Light because his sin would be found out. The man who does what is right comes to the Light. What he does will be seen because he has done what God wanted him to do.*

No matter which side, there are always consequences for our sin. Of course, everyone hates the consequences because it is painful. For true believers, they understand and accept their sin, knowing they are capable of failing and will accept godly counsel and correction. The other avoids acceptance and accountability. I am speaking about those who are trying not to get caught. They do not hate the sin and don't want anyone to find out. 1 Corinthians 10:12 says, *"If you think you are standing strong, be careful not to fall."*

If you think you have falsely repented, there is hope. The Lord is so patient with us, knowing how we struggle: *"The Lord isn't really being slow about his promise, as some people think. No, he is being patient for your sake. He does not want anyone to be destroyed, but wants everyone to repent"* (2 Peter 3:9). He will not reject you when you come to Him with genuine remorse. Read John 6:37: *"However, those the Father has given me will come to me, and I will never reject them."*

THE DIFFERENCE BETWEEN WORKS AND FAITH

Works are all about what you can do to be acceptable to God. You know you are working for acceptance and salvation if you are continually working by your own hands, your thoughts, and decisions to be accepted. This is living with a works mentality. Thoughts like, "If I do this, then God will..." Or, "I need to do more, be kinder, look prettier, get a degree, then God will..." That is all by your hand and a works mentality.

Faith is believing; and believing what you cannot physically see or touch. Faith is accepting without doing anything by your efforts.

But some question works noted in the book of James. They take one sentence and make a religion out of it: *"So you see, we are shown to be right with God by what we do, not by faith alone"* (James 2:24). The King James Version translates the same Scripture as follows: *"Ye see then how that by works a man is justified, and not by faith only."*

Never take one verse to justify or make it what you want it to be. Remember to read Scriptures in their full context. Now read James 2:14-26:

> *What good is it, dear brothers and sisters, if you say you have faith but don't show it by your actions? Can that kind of faith save anyone? Suppose you see a brother or sister who has no food or clothing, and you say, "Goodbye and have a good day; stay warm and eat well"—but*

then you don't give that person any food or clothing. What good does that do? So you see, faith by itself isn't enough. Unless it produces good deeds, it is dead and useless. Now someone may argue, "Some people have faith; others have good deeds." But I say, "How can you show me your faith if you don't have good deeds? I will show you my faith by my good deeds." You say you have faith, for you believe that there is one God. Good for you! Even the demons believe this, and they tremble in terror. How foolish! Can't you see that faith without good deeds is useless? Don't you remember that our ancestor Abraham was shown to be right with God by his actions when he offered his son Isaac on the altar? You see, his faith and his actions worked together. His actions made his faith complete. And so it happened just as the Scriptures say: "Abraham believed God, and God counted him as righteous because of his faith." He was even called the friend of God. So you see, we are shown to be right with God by what we do, not by faith alone. Rahab the prostitute is another example. She was shown to be right with God by her actions when she hid those messengers and sent them safely away by a different road. Just as the body is dead without breath, so also faith is dead without good works.

When you read the Scripture passage in its full context, it makes sense and explains itself. If you genuinely believe, it will show in the things you do. It is by faith in Jesus Christ that we are justified before God. Here they are talking about a relationship between faith and works. They work together hand in hand.

MENTAL ASSENT VERSUS HEART REVELATION

This Scripture is a good illustration of a false convert, especially in verses 15-17. Another lesson we can learn from this Scripture passage is mental assent versus heart revelation. Heart motive is something I believe in strongly. God looks at the heart, and people look at the outward appearance. He says you believe that there is a God, great! Even demons believe there is a God. But do demons demonstrate their belief with actions?

Heart revelation means you have faith and believe; a complete believing and acceptance of something to the point you place all of your trust into it. James has real faith and trust in Christ, not merely believes that He lived on the earth at one time. Many people believe that Jesus lived and walked the planet, but they do not believe He is the Savior or trust Him for forgiveness of sins.

So yes, we are justified by faith; that is, we are made righteous in the eyes of God by faith as revealed in Ephesians 2:8-10:

> ***God saved you by his grace when you believed.*** *And you can't take credit for this; it is a gift from God.* ***Salvation is not a reward for the good things we have done****, so none of us can boast about it. For we are God's masterpiece.* ***He has created us anew in Christ Jesus, so we can do the good things he planned*** *for us long ago.*

When faith is true, it results in deeds relevant to salvation.

Chapter 11

Salvation

If you openly declare that Jesus is Lord and believe in your heart that God raised him from the dead, you will be saved. For it is by believing in your heart that you are made right with God, and it is by openly declaring your faith that you are saved.

—Romans 10:9-10

THE TRUE GOSPEL

Gospel means the teaching or revelation of Christ. Literally the word "gospel" means good news. The good news refers to the story of Jesus Christ's birth, death, and resurrection.

As a minister and teacher of the gospel, there are specific questions I'm asked repeatedly: one being, "How do I know I am truly saved? I said the prayer at church one day, but if I died today, I'm scared I won't be going to Heaven."

Another statement I often hear is, "Well, I try to be a good person," or, "I'm trying to be a good blankly blank." Yikes!

There is no freedom or deliverance in those words. The gospel should bring freedom. These comments are coming from people trying on their efforts to be good enough or acceptable to God: "Hopefully, I'll get to Heaven when I die and be spared going to hell."

Christian "religion" was created by humankind and has messed up things up so much that other religions of the world seem more palatable to people mostly because we have been taught that we need to work for our salvation by our own efforts—be kind enough, good enough, dress right, speak right, and so on. Work, work, work is what many believe to their last breath, and with fingers crossed they hope God will let them into Heaven.

How frightening! I know—I was there. From my youth, I was taught to be obedient or else; and if I'm good, maybe there will be a reward, but the discretion is up to the one giving the reward.

Suppose someone asks you, "If you died today, do you know you would go to Heaven?" Do you stop and second-guess yourself before you answer? Internally do you think, "I don't know"? But outwardly, do you say yes to others? What a horrible injustice has been done! We have taken the precious gospel of Jesus that takes away all fear of death and made it a yoke that is too heavy of a burden to carry.

Other religions in the world are works-focused too. They pray, starve, abuse their bodies, and even kill themselves or others to show their loyalty, believing they will receive a great reward in death. They are working so hard on their own strengths to be acceptable, yet none of these activities bring them even close to any type of salvation. This is what religion has taught us.

Religion is a false gospel conjured up by humans—a list of rules that no one can uphold. From some people's earliest remembrance, they have been taught these ideas, which couldn't be further from the real truth.

The pure gospel of Jesus Christ brings freedom. Religion will kill you. Only the true gospel can save you.

Romans 10:9-10 says,

> *If you openly **declare** that Jesus is Lord and **believe** in your heart that God raised him from the dead, you will be saved. For it is by **believing in your heart** that you are made right with God, and it is by openly declaring your **faith** that **you are saved**.*

What does that mean to be "saved" or "saved by grace"? It means that you have received Jesus, the gift from God, without deserving it. God sent Jesus to die on the cross for the sins of the whole world, so we would not have to pay the price of it on our own. We deserve to go to hell because of our sin. But God made way for us to be spared that by sending Jesus to take the penalty for us.

Jesus is the gift to us from God to receive salvation. It is grace bestowed on us—meaning we don't deserve it, and we can by no means earn it. God has given us His favor, love, and sent His Son to pay for our sins through His death on a cross—even though we are sinners who have done nothing for God. God freely gives His grace to us out of His love for us.

Most of the time, people respond, "Is that all?" Yes, that is all. The gospel is that simple, and salvation is that easy.

The real question is, "Do you believe?" Believing is where people can get stumped. Believing is not as easy as it seems. How do you know that you believe? Salvation is so easy it's hard. Since many have been taught to work to earn, when someone tells us we only have to believe and receive, our minds may stop us and say, "No, that's too easy. I believe I have to have some sort of punishment before being forgiven."

In the Bible, God's Word, Romans 10:9 teaches that you need to *"**declare** that Jesus is Lord and **believe** in your [our] heart."* We can learn something here. God is teaching us that speaking is first, which means that what you speak is very important. That means the more you talk about the Word, the more you will believe in your heart. The Word transforms you from the inside out, not the outside in. Jesus didn't do anything outlandish when He taught people. He sat down and spoke to them with sincerity and authority.

Nowhere in the Scriptures do you find Jesus using any marketing techniques, promises of trips, money, or the like. He sat down and spoke the truth openly to people. And in His talks with His leadership, He never mentioned numbers. He told them to serve. So, are you beginning to see there is a world of difference between the religion taught in some churches today and the real gospel of Jesus? I hope so.

John 16:7-11 talks about Jesus going away and sending to us the Holy Spirit, our Advocate:

> *But in fact, it is best for you that I go away, because if I don't, the Advocate won't come. If I do go away, then I will send*

> *him to you. And when he comes, he will convict the world of its sin, and of God's righteousness, and of the coming judgment. The world's sin is that it refuses to believe in me. Righteousness is available because I go to the Father, and you will see me no more. Judgment will come because the ruler of this world has already been judged.*

The Holy Spirit will show us our sin and lack of right standing with God based on our refusal to believe in Jesus. Notice that the Holy Spirit comes to *"convict the world of its sin."* That means you will be convicted of *your* sin. Not your spouse's sin, or your coworkers' sin, and not all of your sins in life. The Scripture says the Holy Spirit will convict you of your sin of not believing in Him, Jesus.

Notice what Jesus *didn't* say; stop, and reread it! He *didn't* say, "You have to confess to Me all of your sins!" He only mentioned one sin that needs confession—that you did not believe in Him. Jesus is our righteousness. Jesus made us right with God. Not our works of our own hands. Jesus paid for everything on the cross so we would not have to. He knew we could not do it. If we could, there would be no reason for Jesus to pay the price on the cross.

GETTING RIGHT WITH GOD

We get right with God by believing in Jesus and the price He paid so we could be reconciled back into a relationship with God. And it bears explaining, the ruler of this world is speaking of Satan, Jesus has already judged him and conquered him. Jesus went to hell and took everything back that Adam gave up.

Now read again Romans 10:9-13, which tells us exactly how to receive salvation!

> *If you openly **declare** that Jesus is Lord and **believe in your heart** that God raised him from the dead, you will be saved. For it is by believing in your heart that you are made right with God, and it is by openly declaring your **faith** that you are saved. As the Scriptures tell us, "Anyone who **trusts** in him will never be disgraced." Jew and Gentile are the same in this respect. They have the same Lord, who gives generously to all who call on him. For "**Everyone who calls on the name of the LORD will be saved.**"*

Notice God didn't say you have to clean yourself up, quit everything terrible you are doing, and give up all the good things in this life. No, He said to believe in your heart and confess with your mouth that Jesus is Lord. Not mentally agree in your head. No. Believe in your heart.

Now that is the good news! My spirit is excited all over again, just writing this. For one, no one has enough time to confess all the things we've have ever done wrong, and we don't even know all of the things we have ever done wrong. The Word says anything done without faith is a sin: *"Whatever is not from faith is sin"* (Romans 14:23b NKJV). How many times have we done things without faith, but out of fear, doubt, or coercion? That is a sin according to the Scriptures. Thank You, Jesus, for making it simple.

You see, what you believe in your heart will come out through your mouth. So if you have wrong believing and thinking, then your confession is going to be incorrect. Get those three things corrected—believing, thinking, confessing—and your life will change for the better.

Saying you believe is not the issue; it is actually believing. Saying, "I want to lose weight," will not help you, it's the change in your lifestyle that helps you lose weight. Change is a difficult process for most. Human beings for the most part do not like change. Learn to embrace change, because on the other side of that change is freedom. Once you receive the gift of salvation, you are free from the power of sin in your life: *"God has united you with Christ Jesus. For our benefit God made him to be wisdom itself. Christ made us right with God; he made us pure and holy, and **he freed us from sin**"* (1 Corinthians 1:30). The apostle Paul also says in Romans 6:14, **"Sin is no longer your master**, *for you no longer live under the requirements of the law. Instead, you live under the freedom of God's grace."*

You don't have to sin anymore; it has no power over you, unless you allow it. That means when you have the urge to sin, you can say, "NO, I don't have to do that any longer." This was an unknown power to me for a long time. I thought it was just who I was and had to continue the bad habit because I had no control over it. But those Scriptures helped me see that was not true. I can control myself, stop, and say, "No, I am not going to do that."

At first, that was difficult; but the more I did that, the less the urge came back. Don't misunderstand, the flesh is still flesh; and as long as Jesus tarries to return to earth in all His glory, we will have the potential to sin until we come into our glorified bodies.

In the Old Testament, before Jesus, there was the Law of Moses or the Ten Commandments, as you may know it to be. We were under the guardianship of the Law until the way of faith in Jesus came. The Law was given to show people their sin. The Law was only to last until the promised Jesus would come.

Now that Jesus came we no longer need the guardianship of the Law. It is not to say that Jesus came to abolish the law, Jesus fulfilled the requirements of the law. So when you read about the Law in the New Testament, that is what it means. That was the old covenant, and then after Jesus, the Law was done away with and replaced with a new covenant.

The new covenant is God's grace. Romans 7:1-6 explains this. Verse 4 of this chapter says,

> *So, my dear brothers and sisters, this is the point: You died to the power of the law when you died with Christ. And now you are united with the one who was raised from the dead. As a result, we can produce a harvest of good deeds for God.*

We are dead to the law. The law is not bad, but it cannot make you holy. There is no flexibility in it. The law is righteous, but it cannot make you righteous. The law is just, but it cannot justify you. There is the problem. Apostle Paul declared in Romans 7:5, *"When we were controlled by our old nature, sinful desires were at work within us, and the law aroused these evil desires that produced a harvest of sinful deeds, resulting in death."*

So the law arouses simple passions. It does not produce sanctification and holiness. Sanctification and holiness come by faith in Jesus. Jesus is our righteousness, sanctification, and redemption. We have been delivered from the law:

> *But now we have been released from the law, for we died to it and are no longer captive to its power. Now we can serve*

God, not in the old way of obeying the letter of the law, but in the new way of living in the Spirit (Romans 7:6).

The law is performance based and no matter how hard you try it is impossible to fulfill, but Jesus could and did. He has given us a new and better covenant. Now under our new and better covenant we are under grace. Jesus completed all for us.

There is no mixing the two. Do not mix the old covenant with the new covenant. This was the problem that the Galatians had and Paul the Apostle was trying to encourage them not to fall for it. Galatians 1:6 says, *"I am shocked that you are turning away so soon from God, who called you to himself through the loving mercy of Christ. You are following a different way that pretends to be the Good News."*

The religious were trying to convince them that even though they received Jesus, in order to be holy they still needed to abide by the Ten Commandments. This is an error. How is that good news? I already know it is impossible to adhere to the letter of the law. I fail every time. What is the reason for Jesus then? Don't let anyone convince you that once you receive Jesus you still have to fulfill the law. Jesus fulfilled it for us. Let's continue to read Galatians:

But is not the Good News at all. You are being fooled by those who deliberately twist the truth concerning Christ. Let God's curse fall on anyone, including us or even an angel from heaven, who preaches a different kind of Good News than the one we preached to you. I say again what we have said before: If anyone preaches any other Good News than the one you welcomed, let that person be cursed (Galatians 1:7-9).

Apart from the Law, sin is dead. Being under the Law produces bondage, not freedom. And the Law makes you want to sin more. Read 1 Corinthians 15:56: *"For sin is the sting that results in death, and the law gives sin its power."*

The more you say no, the more you want to do it. I won't commit adultery—and what do you want to do? Laying down the law stirs the desire. For example, you have a bucket of water you use to wash your floor. If you let it sit for a while, all the gunk sinks to the bottom of the bucket; the top of the water may look okay, but the gunk is still there sitting at the bottom. But if you take a mop and stir it, what happens? All of that gunk gets stirred up throughout the water and some rises to the top. The law is like the mop. It reawakens evil passions. Now is the mop bad? No! The sediment at the bottom is unclean and unhealthy, the mop only revealed that it is still there.

Read how Paul explains it in Galatians 3:19-22:

> *Why, then, was the law given? It was given alongside the promise to show people their sins. But the law was designed to last only until the coming of the child who was promised. God gave his law through angels to Moses, who was the mediator between God and the people. Now a mediator is helpful if more than one party must reach an agreement. But God, who is one, did not use a mediator when he gave his promise to Abraham. Is there a conflict, then, between God's law and God's promises? Absolutely not! If the law could give us new life, we could be made right with God by obeying it. But the* **Scriptures declare that we are all prisoners of sin, so we receive God's promise of freedom only by believing in Jesus Christ.**

Back then, the Law was the mediator between God and the people; today, Jesus is the Mediator between God and the people (1 Timothy 2:5). Now read Romans 7:7-12:

Well then, am I suggesting that the law of God is sinful? Of course not! In fact, it was the law that showed me my sin. I would never have known that coveting is wrong if the law had not said, "You must not covet." But sin used this command to arouse all kinds of covetous desires within me! If there were no law, sin would not have that power. At one time I lived without understanding the law. But when I learned the command not to covet, for instance, the power of sin came to life, and I died. So I discovered that the law's commands, which were supposed to bring life, brought spiritual death instead. Sin took advantage of those commands and deceived me; it used the commands to kill me. But still, the law itself is holy, and its commands are holy and right and good.

There are many preachers still teaching that you must obey the Ten Commandments even after salvation. That is not true. The Ten Commandments are not for the saved but the unsaved. Why would you want to go back into bondage when you have been set free from bondage? This teaching is nothing new since they had this problem at the beginning of the church. The religious leaders were trying to force new believers into continuing to obey the law. The law produced a works mentality. There was a list of right and wrongs; and if you broke one of them, you were guilty of them all! Who can keep that? Anyone who teaches that today is placing you back under bondage after you have been freed from these things. Why go back and try to earn your salvation through your efforts?

The story of Sarah and Hagar is another illustration to further explain law versus grace. If you are not familiar with it, you can read their full story in Genesis 16. In the example, Hagar represents the law, and Sarah represents grace. Paul talks about the difference between the two women and their sons in Galatians 4:21-31:

> *Tell me, you who want to live under the law, do you know what the law actually says? The Scriptures say that Abraham had two sons, one from his slave wife and one from his freeborn wife. The son of the slave wife was born in a human attempt to bring about the fulfillment of God's promise. But the son of the freeborn wife was born as God's own fulfillment of his promise. These two women serve as an illustration of God's two covenants. The first woman, Hagar, represents Mount Sinai where people received the law that enslaved them. And now Jerusalem is just like Mount Sinai in Arabia, because she and her children live in slavery to the law. But the other woman, Sarah, represents the heavenly Jerusalem. She is the free woman, and she is our mother. As Isaiah said, "Rejoice, O childless woman, you who have never given birth! Break into a joyful shout, you who have never been in labor! For the desolate woman now has more children than the woman who lives with her husband!" And you, dear brothers and sisters, are children of the promise, just like Isaac. But you are now being persecuted by those who want you to keep the law, just as Ishmael, the child born by human effort, persecuted Isaac, the child born by the power of the Spirit. But what do the Scriptures say about that? "Get rid of the slave and her son, for the son of the slave woman will not share the inheritance with the free woman's son."*

So, dear brothers and sisters, we are not children of the slave woman; we are children of the free woman.

What he is saying is that God's children are to live under the blessings of grace and no longer under the bondage of the Law.

You no longer need the Law to become Christlike because you are already complete in Christ. Religion makes it sound right, but it is not. That is why you need to learn who you are now in Jesus Christ.

Colossians 2:8-23 say,

Don't let anyone capture you with empty philosophies and high-sounding nonsense that come from human thinking and from the spiritual powers of this world, rather than from Christ. For in Christ lives all the fullness of God in a human body. So you also are complete through your union with Christ, who is the head over every ruler and authority. When you came to Christ, you were "circumcised," but not by a physical procedure. Christ performed a spiritual circumcision—the cutting away of your sinful nature. For you were buried with Christ when you were baptized. And with him you were raised to new life because you trusted the mighty power of God, who raised Christ from the dead. You were dead because of your sins and because your sinful nature was not yet cut away. Then God made you alive with Christ, for he forgave all our sins. He canceled the record of the charges against us and took it away by nailing it to the cross. In this way, he disarmed the spiritual rulers and authorities. He shamed them publicly by his victory over them on the cross. So don't let anyone condemn you for what you eat or drink, or for not celebrating certain holy days or new moon ceremonies or Sabbaths. For these rules are only shadows of the reality yet to come. And Christ himself is that reality. Don't let anyone condemn you by insisting on pious self-denial or the worship of angels, saying they have had visions about these things. Their sinful minds have made them proud, and they are not connected to Christ, the head of the body. For he holds the whole body together with its joints and ligaments, and it grows as God nourishes it. You have died with Christ, and he has set you free from the spiritual powers of this world. So why do you keep on following the rules of the world, such as, "Don't handle! Don't taste! Don't touch!"? Such rules are mere human teachings about things that deteriorate as we use them. These rules may seem wise because they require strong devotion, pious self-denial, and severe bodily discipline. But they provide no help in conquering a person's evil desires.

What if you have broken your relationship with God? There is a confession of sin for a believer who broke fellowship with God. Read 1 John 1:3-10:

We proclaim to you what we ourselves have actually seen and heard so that you may have fellowship with us. And our fellowship is with the Father and with his Son, Jesus Christ. We are writing these things so that you may fully share our joy. This is the message we heard from Jesus and now declare to you: God is light, and there is no darkness in him at all. So we are lying if we say we have fellowship with God but go on living in spiritual darkness; we are not practicing the truth. But if we are living in the light, as God is in the light, then we have fellowship with each other, and the blood of Jesus, his

Son, cleanses us from all sin. If we claim we have no sin, we are only fooling ourselves and not living in the truth. But if we confess our sins to him, he is faithful and just to forgive us our sins and to cleanse us from all wickedness. If we claim we have not sinned, we are calling God a liar and showing that his word has no place in our hearts.

This Scripture from 1 John is speaking to believers, not unbelievers. Remember, the New Testament is for people who already claim Jesus as Lord and Savior. The New Testament is written to the believers in Jesus Christ. Don't take it out of context.

Unbelievers do not have a fellowship with God; only believers do. This is for believers who have sinned and know it but deny it. You know you are doing things that are not of love. Things such as backbiting, gossiping, slandering, stealing, gluttony, adultery, pornography, and the list goes on. God still loves you, except you slowly pull away from Him little by little out of shame and guilt. Your spirit knows it is not right. It is not who you are any longer. Religion may have taught you that grace allows you to do anything and everything you want, and you will still go to Heaven. Don't be so shallow to believe that. Your spirit says otherwise. Consider now Romans 6:1-4:

*Well then, **should we keep on sinning** so that God can show us more and more of his wonderful grace? **Of course not!** Since we have died to sin, how can we continue to live in it? Or have you forgotten that when we were joined with Christ Jesus in baptism, we joined him in his death? For we died and were buried with Christ by baptism. And just as Christ was raised from* *the dead by the glorious power of the Father,* **now we also may live new lives.**

God is telling you how to reconcile your fellowship with Him. You reconcile it by confessing. Sin has lost its power over you and your life. You do not have to sin anymore. You can say no to those sinful habits and walk away from them.

So today, if you are reading this and feeling convicted, don't wait! Put the book down and confess it and reconnect your relationship with the Lord—then come back to the book. Remember: *"But if we confess our sins to him,* **he is faithful and just to forgive us** *our sins and to cleanse us from all wickedness"* (1 John 1:9).

You can say, "I can't help it; it's just who I am," or, "God knows my heart." These are excuses to allow us to continue in something we don't hate or want to let go of in our lives, which will keep you exactly where you are and stunt your spiritual growth. Then 30 years later, as you are the same person sucked dry from the issues of life, you will be blaming God instead of placing blame where it should be.

Once you accept the gift of Jesus, the Bible doesn't leave you there. It teaches you who you are now and how to conduct yourself as a child of the Most High God. Reading the Word reveals how to make decisions, love your enemies, what behaviors to deal with, and that you are an heir to God's Kingdom. God our Father wants to teach us everything that brings us life.

It seems that not many in the church today want to teach us what we need to know. And as individuals, many don't want to go any further in their relationship with Christ.

Some make their relationship a get-out-of-hell-free card by abusing grace. Some who may read this book are standing proud saying, "I am right—you are wrong." Except for what this Scripture tells us,

> *Everything is pure to those whose hearts are pure. But nothing is pure to those who are corrupt and unbelieving, because their minds and consciences are corrupted. Such people claim they know God, but they deny him by the way they live. They are detestable and disobedient, worthless for doing anything good* (Titus 1:15-16).

Religion teaches it is okay not to have heart revelation, but what does light have to do with darkness? You are the *light* of the world, and evil behaviors are part of the darkness.

Before finishing, let me add that there is a place for the Law today. The Law shows us our sin, and it can be used in bringing those who are not saved to Jesus Christ. On the one hand, the law is a mirror to show us our sinful state and ourselves. The mirror can also show the glory of Jesus.

When you wash your face, you are not looking in the mirror, you have your head down focused on the washing with soap and water. That is the power of the Word of God. When you keep your face in the Word and learn who you are, when you lift your head and look in the mirror, you will see your transformation as you become more like Him.

Any church that teaches you the law is not teaching the true gospel of the grace of God that is in Jesus Christ. The true gospel brings freedom: *"For the Lord is the Spirit, and* **wherever the Spirit of the Lord is, there is freedom"** (2 Corinthians 3:17).

Also, consider what Jesus said in John 8:31-36:

> *Jesus said to the people who **believed** in him, "You are truly my disciples if you **remain faithful to my teachings**. And you will know the truth, and **the truth will set you free**." "But we are descendants of Abraham," they said. "We have never been slaves to anyone. What do you mean, 'You will be set free'?" Jesus replied, "I tell you the truth, everyone who sins is a slave of sin. A slave is not a permanent member of the family, but a son is part of the family forever. So if the Son sets you free, **you are truly free**".*

This is the good news! You do not have to fear death any longer if you belong to Jesus. John 5:24 says, *"I tell you the truth, those who **listen** to my message and **believe** in God who sent me have eternal life. They will **never be condemned for their sins, but they have already passed from death into life.**"*

Closing

"For I know the plans I have for you," says the LORD. "They are plans for good and not for disaster, to give you a future and a hope."
—Jeremiah 29:11

Part of my endless pursuit in this life is something I learned from the apostle John. In the Gospel of John, which he wrote, we find him referring to himself as the disciple *"whom Jesus loved."* To some this may sound boastful as he declares himself to be loved by Jesus, perhaps insinuating that the others were not as favored as he.

To me, there are very few deep relationships in the Scriptures such as the one between John and Jesus. There were close friends such as David and Jonathan, Lazarus and Jesus. And Mary, who chose to forget everything else and sit at the feet of Jesus, which was a different demeanor than her sister Martha had. My thought of John is one of rest. He was to me a quiet man with a big heart, an introverted thinker, and resolved yet bold when needed.

John knew without a doubt that Jesus loved him; and at the Lord's supper, he laid his head on the chest of Jesus. Each apostle had a different personality, but not one of them was like John. Peter was outspoken, abrupt, harsh at times, and lacked a filter in what he said. Thomas needed proof to believe. John, on the other hand, knew something the others had not yet learned—to believe, trust, and rest in the love that Jesus had for him.

John knew that Jesus loved him, and he rested on that. John loved Jesus and perhaps was such a comfort to Jesus. I can see him listening intently and taking in every word that Jesus taught. It seems to me that John's heart was warm and pure with love for everyone, stemming from the love he knew Jesus had for him. I believe John knew and relished in the fact that Jesus loved him so much.

And John's pure, sincere love would be something that Jesus could find comforting and refreshing, considering all the people He encountered. As John rested on the chest of Jesus and listened to His heartbeat, it didn't seem to matter what others thought; he didn't seem distracted by all the goings on and conversations.

Like Mary at Jesus's feet who chose to sit and listen, John trusted and rested in the love of Jesus—and that is my goal. From all the distractions in this life, may I ever find solace, rest, love, acceptance, peace, and joy just sitting and listening, trusting and resting in His love for me. To continually learn to lean back on the chest of Jesus and be taken away by His heartbeat so the whole world fades away, and all that matters is Him. Thinking and imagining that brings a thankful sigh to my heart.

For you, my prayer is what Paul would pray for those reading his letters:

May the God who gives endurance and encouragement give you the same attitude of mind toward each other that Christ Jesus had, so that with one heart and one voice you may glorify the God and Father of our Lord Jesus Christ....May the God of hope fill you with all joy and peace as you trust in him, so that you may overflow with hope by the power of the Holy Spirit (Romans 15:5-6,13 NIV).

Shalom

About the Author

Barbara King knows firsthand what it means to rise from the vestiges of brokenness. Her incredible journey has led her to serve the Lord for more than three decades.

She is a noted author and a prolific teacher with a special passion for the Ministry of Helps. She is an educator who has served as an associate professor with Eagle's Wings Bible Institute in Chicago.

Barbara serves on the board of directors for Eagle's Wings International, a global apostolic ministry. She holds a Bachelor of Theology degree and a Master's degree in Church Administration from Life Christian University in Florida, USA. She is currently completing her Doctorate in Ministry with THE 300, a California-based global ministry training college.

Barbara King resides in Murfreesboro, Tennessee.

Eagle's Wings PRESS

Get in touch with us:
EAGLE'S WINGS INTERNATIONAL

PO Box 6295, McKinney TX 75071, USA
Email: office@e-wings.net

- **f** /ddsempebwa
- **◉** /drdennissempebwa
- **🐦** /dsempebwa
- **in** /in/dennis-sempebwa-d-min-phd